Fabulous
FOOD

LYNN BEDFORD HALL

ACKNOWLEDGEMENTS

Once again it's the same team that approved, edited and sent most of my previous books on their happy way. As before, I regard Linda de Villiers, Joy Clack and Bev Dodd as a formidable trio. They will offer praise when they think it is due, but will gently disagree when they don't go along with my ideas. This makes for perfect interaction and, in the end, they usually know best because they are true publishing, editing and design professionals – a rare threesome, and I cannot imagine where else I would find colleagues with the same amount of care and dedicated involvement. My sincere thanks to Nelani Pfaff, who so expertly edited the Afrikaans edition; and to Justine and Ryno for their inspired interpretations of my work. Their combined expertise is evident on every page.

First published in 2007 by Struik Publishers
(a division of New Holland Publishing (South Africa) (Pty) Ltd)
Cape Town • London • Sydney • Auckland

www.struik.co.za

Cornelis Struik House, 80 McKenzie Street,
Cape Town 8001, South Africa
Garfield House, 86–88 Edgware Road, London W2 2EA,
United Kingdom
14 Aquatic Drive, Frenchs Forest, NSW 2086, Australia
218 Lake Road, Northcote, Auckland, New Zealand

New Holland Publishing is a member of Johnnic
Communications Ltd

PUBLISHING MANAGER: Linda de Villiers
EDITOR: Joy Clack
DESIGNER: Beverley Dodd
PHOTOGRAPHER: Ryno
STYLIST: Justine Drake
PROOFREADER: Tessa Kennedy

Reproduction by Hirt & Carter Cape (Pty) Ltd
Printed and bound by Craft Print International Pte Ltd,
Singapore

ISBN 9 781770 073647

www.imagesofafrica.co.za

IMAGES OF AFRICA
PHOTO LIBRARY

Over 40 000 unique African images available to purchase
from our image bank at **www.imagesofafrica.co.za**

The publishers wish to thank the following outlets for their
assistance and for the loan of props for the photography:
@ Home; Banks; Boardmans; Brighthouse; Clicks;
The Culinary Academy; Home etc.; James Russel Agencies;
Le Creuset; Loads of Living; Loft Living; L'Orangerie;
Silk & Cotton Company; Silwood Kitchen School of Cookery;
Wallflower; Woolworths; Yellow Door.

CONTENTS

AUTHOR'S INTRODUCTION

Most of us who love to cook will agree that a photograph of a completed dish sends out an exciting signal; not only does it inspire confidence, it also provides guidance: you no longer have to say 'What On Earth Will My Dish Look Like?' In short, a photograph will speak to you, whereas a picture in the mind can simply be a wobbly confusion, especially for the timid cook.

Now with this book you no longer have to draw on your creative ability to produce what you think the author had in mind, because, at a glance, you will know what to expect: a succulent curry, a glistening salad, a steaming soup. Follow the photograph and your troubles should be over. Most of the recipes featured in *Fig Jam and Foxtrot* and *Return to Corriebush* reappear here in colour. To add balance and variety, some recipes from my books that are now out-of-print have been included, together with a smattering of timeless favourites and new inspirations. So whether you just look – or look and then cook – I do hope you will find pleasure in browsing through these pages.

LYNN BEDFORD HALL

SOUPS
hot and cold

CUCUMBER AND AVOCADO soup on ice

This is a thick and gorgeous soup, so smooth and rich that it needs no extras, not even a cobweb of cream.

The garnish, so to speak, comes in the form of little dill fronds frozen in ice cubes.

1 x 550–600 g English cucumber (that's a big one)

15 ml (1 Tbsp) each oil and butter

2 medium leeks, chopped

1 medium onion, chopped

500 ml (2 cups) hot chicken stock

a small clutch of parsley tufts

2 bay leaves

a little sea salt

2 medium or 1 jumbo avocado, diced (300 g flesh, once peeled and pipped), reserve the pip

2–3 small fronds of fresh dill

15 ml (1 Tbsp) fresh lime juice

finely grated rind of ½ small lime

Pare the cucumber, cut in half and remove the seeds, then dice. Heat the oil and butter in a deep saucepan, add the leeks and onion and cook slowly until soft and transparent. Mix in the cucumber and cook briefly until it has started to shrink a little. Add the stock, parsley, bay leaves and salt, then cover and simmer for about 25 minutes until the vegetables are very soft. Leave to cool, then remove the bay leaves. Add the avocado flesh, the dill, lime juice and rind, and whizz in a blender until beautifully thick and smooth. Pour into a large glass jug, drop in the avocado pip, then cover and refrigerate for at least 6 hours, or even overnight.

During this time, make the dilled ice cubes. Empty an ice cube tray and, in the hollows, place a small frond of dill, fill up with water, and freeze. Use a tray with small, round hollows or, if yours makes large cubes, only half-fill them with water, otherwise the cubes will take too long to melt. Before serving, remove the avo pip, check the seasoning, give the soup a good stir and pour into small bowls (not soup plates). Drop one or two dilly ice cubes into each bowl, then go away for a few minutes to allow them to just start melting before serving. **Serves 6–8.**

CHILLED BEETROOT SOUP with avocado cream

Imagine a bowl of incredibly vivid, magenta-coloured soup, floated with avocado and swirled with cream, and you've got this colourful wonder. It's a fun soup, and easy to make because the ingredients are so basic.

15 ml (1 Tbsp) each oil and butter
1 medium onion, sliced into thin rings
2 large leeks, white part only, well washed and chopped
15 ml (1 Tbsp) water
450–500 g potatoes, peeled and cubed
2 ml (½ tsp) each grated nutmeg and paprika
1 litre (4 cups) hot chicken stock
2 bay leaves
a little sea salt
a good pinch of sugar
2 medium, raw beetroot, peeled and coarsely grated
(about 230 g peeled weight)
125 ml (½ cup) milk
a little fresh lemon juice
white vermouth (optional)
softly whipped cream (or thick sour cream or creamy
Greek yoghurt), and cubed or balled avocado, and
milled black pepper – these are not just garnishes,
they are essentials

Heat the oil and butter in a really large saucepan (because grated beetroot is bulky), and add the onion and leeks. Toss until coated, then add the water and sweat, covered, over very low heat until soft and golden; do not brown. Add the potatoes, nutmeg and paprika, toss to mix, then add the stock, bay leaves, seasoning and beetroot. Cover and simmer very gently until the vegetables are cooked – about 25 minutes. Remove from heat, stir in the milk and, when reasonably cool, whizz in a blender, in batches, until smooth. Check the seasoning – if it needs a little oomph, shake in a few drops of lemon juice. Refrigerate. To serve, ladle into soup bowls. If using vermouth, it goes in before the garnish – just a dash. Spoon a large dollop of cream on top, gently mix in a generous helping of the cubed or balled avocado, then grind over a little black pepper.
Serves 6–8.

MINTED CUCUMBER AND YOGHURT soup with walnuts

*A thoroughly unusual soup, pale and creamy and crunchy all at the same time. In fact, it might cause
a bit of a skrik at the first sip, because it's so different from chilled, creamy soups. But it's really good,
and if you're looking for something quite different and refreshing with which to start off a meal
on a hot summer's evening, this one could hit just the right spot.*

500 g English cucumber
375 ml (1½ cups) stirred Bulgarian yoghurt
(not thick yoghurt)
1 small clove garlic, chopped
1 slim spring onion, chopped
125 ml (½ cup) thin cream
**8 small to medium fresh mint leaves (avoid the large
older ones)**
sugar to taste and a pinch of sea salt
chopped walnuts to garnish

Pare the cucumber, slice into long strips, flick out all
the seeds, then cut into small cubes. You should have
400 g. Poach in a little salted water over low heat –
use a wide-based frying pan so that the cubes can be
spread out – until soft and translucent. Watch that the
water doesn't boil away – add a little more if it looks
dry before the cucumber is soft. When done, drain if
necessary, then purée in a blender with the yoghurt,
garlic, spring onion, cream and mint – the mixture
should be smooth, creamy and lightly flecked with
green. Before removing from the blender, taste – it
will need a little sugar and perhaps a pinch of salt or
another mint leaf or two. Chill overnight in a glass
container, loosely covered. Before serving, check
seasoning – if the flavour is too tart, stir in a little
runny honey – it makes all the difference. Into each
small chilled soup cup place 30 ml (2 Tbsp) cucumber
cubes (prepared as above), pour in some soup,
scatter with walnuts and serve. **Serves 4–5 and is
easily doubled.**

CHILLED SPANSPEK soup

It's slightly spicy, slightly sweet, most unusual and quite delicious. Make it in the hot summer months when spanspeks (sweet melons) are at their peak.

30 ml (2 Tbsp) oil
5 ml (1 tsp) butter
1 medium onion, chopped
2 leeks, white part only, sliced
7 ml (1½ tsp) mild curry powder
2 ml (½ tsp) turmeric
a tiny knob of fresh root ginger, peeled and grated
1 stick cinnamon
1 whole star anise
1 small, ripe and bright spanspek, peeled and cubed
(500 g prepared weight)
500 ml (2 cups) lightly seasoned chicken stock
250 ml (1 cup) milk
fresh lemon juice
thin, pouring cream and fresh coriander to garnish

Heat the oil and butter in a large saucepan, add the onion and leeks and allow to soften without browning. Add the spices and stir for a minute over low heat. Add the melon cubes, toss to mix, then add the stock. Cover and simmer over very low heat for about 15 minutes, until the melon cubes are very soft. Set aside to cool. Remove and discard the cinnamon and anise, then add the milk and purée in a blender until smooth – do this in batches. Check the seasoning and add a little lemon juice, just enough to sharpen the flavour. Pour into a fridge container, cover and refrigerate until icy cold, or up to 24 hours. To serve, pour into individual chilled soup cups, add a drizzle of cream to each – swirl into a cobweb, using a skewer – then scatter with a few fresh coriander leaves. **Serves 6**.

CAULIFLOWER VICHYSSOISE
with nutmeg and lemon

This is a slightly different version of the classic creamy potato and leek soup, offering a new taste without altogether changing the character of the original, and a good choice when you need a soup that's unfailingly popular, quick to make, and doesn't require a shopping trip because the ingredients are already in your pantry. Although vichyssoise is traditionally served cold, chilling does tend to dull the flavour, and this one is best served hot.

30 ml (2 Tbsp) each oil and butter

2 medium onions, chopped

4 large leeks, white part only, chopped

700 g potatoes, peeled and cubed

500 g cauliflower florets

7 ml (1½ tsp) freshly grated nutmeg

4 x 4 cm strips lemon peel

2 litres (8 cups) hot chicken stock

4 bay leaves

sea salt to taste

125 ml (½ cup) each milk and thick cream

fresh lemon juice (optional)

snipped fresh chives to garnish

Heat the oil and butter in a large saucepan, add the onions and leeks and sweat over low heat, shaking the pan occasionally and taking care that the vegetables do not brown. When soft and pale, add the potatoes, cauliflower and nutmeg and toss to mix, then add the lemon peel, stock, bay leaves and salt. Cover and simmer until the vegetables are soft – about 25 minutes. Leave to cool down a bit, remove the bay leaves and lemon peel, then purée in a blender, in batches, until smooth. Return to the saucepan, add the milk and cream and reheat, stirring, without boiling. Check seasoning – the soup might need a little more salt, and a squeeze of lemon juice to sharpen the flavour. Ladle into warmed soup bowls and sprinkle with chives. **Serves 8–10.**

QUICK GAZPACHO
with whipped basil cream

A speedy version of the popular Spanish summer soup, using a method which, although not traditional,
puts it within reach of the busiest cook. Normally, gazpacho is served with chopped salad ingredients and croûtons –
but a surprising topping of savoury cream gives the old favourite a new look and a smoother flavour.
Serve in plain white bowls to show off the contrasting colours.

2 x 2 cm thick slices crustless bread
600 g ripe tomatoes, skinned, seeded and chopped
1 large English cucumber, pared, seeded and chopped
1 fat clove garlic, chopped
1 large leek, white part only, chopped
400 ml (1⅗ cups) tomato juice (not tomato cocktail)
5 ml (1 tsp) each sea salt and sugar
15 ml (1 Tbsp) red wine vinegar
30 ml (2 Tbsp) olive oil
1 red pepper, seeded, ribs removed, and chopped

BASIL CREAM
125 ml (½ cup) cream
about 10 fresh basil leaves, torn
a pinch each of sea salt and paprika

Soak the bread briefly in a little water and squeeze dry, then mix with the remaining ingredients in a large bowl. Spoon into a blender and purée in batches until almost smooth. Do not expect a velvety result – although the vegetables should be completely pulped, the mixture will appear mushy and rather thick. This is correct, as gazpacho is served over ice cubes, which thin it down a little. Turn into a fridge container and chill. The soup should be served after about 2 hours, but will hold for longer if necessary.

For the basil cream, whisk together all the ingredients until fairly thick, then chill until needed. Give the soup a good stir before serving, and check seasoning. Pour into chilled bowls over a cube or two of ice, and top each serving with a dollop of basil cream – either left in a big blob, or swirled into a cobweb. **Serves 8.**

MUSHROOM, LEEK AND BARLEY broth

The title may sound pedestrian, but this is a soup unlike any other: earthy and intense, with a slightly smoky fragrance, it is quite different from the usual creamy mushroom soups. This version requires the mushrooms to 'mull' for an hour or so in red wine, while the colour and flavour gather depth. The addition of leeks and barley gives a nod to Scotland, the quince jelly adds a surprising local touch, and the final blend is simply a lovely comfort soup for a chilly night.

125 ml (½ cup) pearled barley

2 medium onions, finely chopped

4 large leeks, shredded

60 ml (4 Tbsp) butter

2 medium carrots, finely diced

500 g brown mushrooms, wiped and chopped

250 ml (1 cup) red wine (claret is a good choice)

5 ml (1 tsp) freshly grated nutmeg

2 litres (8 cups) chicken stock*

20 ml (4 tsp) tomato paste

sea salt to taste

20 ml (4 tsp) quince jelly

a little chopped fresh parsley

Rinse the barley and soak in water to cover for 45 minutes. Meanwhile, place the onions, leeks, butter, carrots, mushrooms, wine and nutmeg in a large, deep saucepan. Bring to the boil, then cook briskly, uncovered, stirring until the liquid has reduced to a few bubbles and the vegetables start to darken. Now add the stock, tomato paste, salt and the drained barley and, when boiling, reduce the heat, cover and simmer gently for at least 1 hour, stirring now and then. Check the seasoning, swirl in the jelly and parsley, then leave the soup to stand for 10 minutes before serving, while it thickens to maximum, and all the flavours come together. Ladle into deep, warmed bowls. **Serves 8.**

* Next time you roast a chicken, make a stock from the carcass – a home-made stock makes all the difference here.

BUTTERNUT AND SWEET POTATO soup

The addition of fresh ginger at the end adds an elusive zing to this gently glowing old favourite.

15 ml (1 Tbsp) oil

a small knob of butter

1 large onion, finely chopped

2 ml (½ tsp) each freshly grated nutmeg,
ground cinnamon and turmeric

500 g butternut, peeled and diced (prepared weight)

250 g peeled, diced, red-skinned sweet potatoes
(prepared weight)

2 medium Golden Delicious apples, peeled and diced

1 litre (4 cups) hot chicken or vegetable stock

2 bay leaves

sea salt to taste

30 ml (2 Tbsp) coarsely grated, peeled root ginger

250 ml (1 cup) milk

fresh lemon juice and honey (optional)

thin cream (optional)

Heat the oil and butter in a large saucepan, add the onion and, when turning golden, add the spices, tossing until aromatic. As the spices absorb excess oil, add a little water to prevent scorching – keep the heat low. Add the vegetables and apples. Toss to mix with the spices and to colour them a little, then add the stock, bay leaves and salt. (This quantity of liquid may seem very little, but the apples add their juices and there's still some milk to come.) Cover and simmer very gently until soft – about 25 minutes – adding the ginger a few minutes before the end of the cooking time. Cool, remove the bay leaves, then purée in a blender until smooth; you will need to do this in two or more batches. Return to the saucepan, stir in the milk, and taste – it might need more salt, a dash of lemon juice, or even a trickle of honey. Reheat, stirring. If making the soup in advance, don't reheat – pour into a container with a lid and refrigerate overnight.

To serve, pour the hot soup into heated bowls. It would be a pity to mask the spicy character with a flavoursome garnish, but a little thin cream in the centre of each serving is good. Drop in a teaspoonful and swirl the cream around. **Serves 8.**

BUTTERNUT, BUTTER BEAN,
coconut and basmati soup

The list of ingredients might look intimidating, but don't be fazed because this soup is really easy, amazingly good, and you won't need a main course afterwards.

125 ml (½ cup) basmati rice

1 ml (¼ tsp) turmeric

30 ml (2 Tbsp) oil

1 large onion, finely chopped

1 large butternut, peeled and cut into small dice
   (600 g prepared weight)

300 g carrots, diced

7 ml (1½ tsp) ground cumin

5 ml (1 tsp) ground coriander

4 cm piece fresh root ginger, peeled and coarsely grated

2 stalks lemon grass, white part only, bruised (optional)

1 x 400 ml can coconut milk (regular or lite)

250 ml (1 cup) chicken stock

a little sea salt

1 x 400 g can butter beans, drained and rinsed

a large handful of fresh coriander leaves

fresh lemon juice

garam masala

Cook the basmati rice as usual, adding the turmeric to the cooking water. When done, cover and leave. You can reheat it if working ahead – add a little water, heat gently, and loosen with a fork.

For the soup, heat the oil in a large saucepan and sauté the onion until golden (adding a pinch of sugar helps, as there is no butter to add colour). Add the vegetables, spices and ginger and toss until aromatic. Add the lemon grass, coconut milk, stock and salt. Cover and simmer until the vegetables are soft – 45 minutes. If the vegetables are still chunky, remove the lemon grass, then use a potato masher to reduce the veg – not too much, leave some texture. Add the beans and coriander and heat through, then add just enough lemon juice to sharpen the taste. If the soup is too thick, add a little more stock. Ladle into heated bowls. Gently place a large spoonful of rice in the centre. Dust with garam masala, and serve with hot naan bread. **Serves 4 and, if doubling up, use an enormous saucepan.**

ROASTED PUMPKIN SOUP
with rooibos and spices

It's the colour of a full moon glazed by the setting sun – deep orange, smooth and beautiful. The ingredients, however, are quite basic, with a little of South Africa's famous brew adding an elusive touch.

600 g firm-fleshed, bright orange pumpkin, peeled and cubed (prepared weight)
30 ml (2 Tbsp) olive oil
10 ml (2 tsp) light brown sugar
3 ml (generous ½ tsp) ground cinnamon
2 medium carrots, sliced
1 medium apple, peeled and chopped
1 medium potato, peeled and cubed
1 very large onion, chopped
2 ml (½ tsp) each paprika and ground ginger
3 whole cloves
500 ml (2 cups) chicken stock
sea salt and a little white pepper
500 ml (2 cups) hot rooibos tea made with 2 teabags
250 ml (1 cup) milk or half milk/half thin cream
fresh lemon juice
no garnish necessary, but you might just put a nasturtium on the side plate

Toss the pumpkin cubes with the oil, sugar and cinnamon until coated, then spread out in a single layer on a baking tray lined with baking paper. Roast at 200 °C for 25–30 minutes or until sizzling and beginning to colour.
Mix the carrots, apple, potato, onion and spices in a large, deep saucepan. Using a slotted spoon, remove the pumpkin from the baking tray and add to the saucepan. Add the stock, seasoning and the hot tea, bring to the boil, then immediately reduce the heat, cover and simmer slowly until all the vegetables are cooked and soft – about 30 minutes. Cool, remove the cloves and then purée in a blender, in batches, until absolutely smooth. The mixture will be very thick. If working ahead, it may be refrigerated for a day. To reheat, add the milk or milk and cream, and bring just to boiling point. Taste, and if it needs sharpening, add a squeeze of lemon juice. **Serves 6.**

AROMATIC DHAL soup

A delicious mix of textures and spicy flavours mingle exuberantly in this ochre-coloured soup.
It's both easy and economical, and looks really inviting served in white soup bowls.

30 ml (2 Tbsp) each oil and butter

2 medium onions, chopped

3 cloves garlic, crushed

2 sticks cinnamon

5 ml (1 tsp) ground cumin

10 ml (2 tsp) each ground coriander and turmeric

500 ml (2 cups) red lentils, rinsed and drained

2 litres (8 cups) chicken stock

a little sea salt and sugar

30 ml (2 Tbsp) tomato paste

1 medium potato (125 g), peeled and coarsely grated

thick Bulgarian yoghurt, garam masala and fresh
   coriander leaves to garnish

Heat the oil and butter in a large saucepan. Add the onions and garlic and, when softening, add the spices. Allow them to sizzle for a minute or two over low heat, adding a dash of water if necessary to prevent scorching. Add the remaining ingredients, except the garnish, bring to the boil, then cover and simmer gently, stirring occasionally, for about 25 minutes or until the lentils and potato are soft and the ingredients have cooked almost to a purée. Stir vigorously to combine and, if too thick, add a little more stock. Check seasoning, remove and discard the cinnamon, and spoon the soup into warmed bowls. Top each serving with a dollop of yoghurt, sprinkle with garam masala, and surround with a few coriander leaves. **Serves 8–10.**

BEAN, PASTA AND VEGETABLE soup

Using a can of beans instead of soaking and cooking haricots is a clever short cut, and means that in just one hour you can have a substantial meal-in-a-soup at very little cost. A teaspoon of pesto swirled into each serving adds a marvellous zip to the flavour, but if you don't have pesto, pass freshly grated or shaved pecorino for sprinkling. Serve with a loaf of crusty bread and a carafe of red wine. Perfect for a wintry Sunday supper, and no main course needed after this.

30 ml (2 Tbsp) oil
2 onions, chopped
2 cloves garlic, crushed
3–4 carrots, diced
3 sticks celery, plus some leaves, sliced
2 litres (8 cups) chicken or vegetable stock
125 ml (½ cup) tomato purée
a handful of fresh flat-leaf parsley, chopped
about 5 ml (1 tsp) sea salt
a large pinch of sugar
1 x 420 g can baked beans in tomato sauce
250 ml (1 cup) elbow macaroni
750 ml (3 cups) finely shredded spinach leaves
(ribs removed)
2 ml (½ tsp) dried oregano

Heat the oil in a large saucepan, add the onions and garlic and soften without browning. Add the carrots and celery and stir-fry briefly. Add the stock, tomato purée, parsley and seasoning. Cover and simmer gently for about 25 minutes, until the vegetables are cooked. Add the remaining ingredients, return to the boil, then cover and simmer over low heat for 30 minutes, stirring occasionally to prevent sticking – you might have to add a little extra stock. Check seasoning, ladle into deep, warmed soup bowls, and garnish each serving as suggested above. **Serves 8.**

CHUNKY VEGETABLE PASTA SOUP
with pesto toasts

A really robust soup and spot-on for supper on a cold night. The addition of borlotti beans is optional –
if unobtainable, use cannellinis. The pesto toasts are not served separately, but plopped into the bowls before
adding the soup, and the whole affair adds up to a buxom, full-flavoured meal-in-a-bowl. Finish off with
a leafy salad, or fresh fruit, or lovely, munchy biscotti with coffee.

30 ml (2 Tbsp) olive oil

1 large onion, finely chopped

3 cloves garlic, crushed

2 sticks celery (remove any stringy sides), plus leaves, chopped

2 medium carrots, diced

200 g courgettes (baby marrows), pared and diced

5 ml (1 tsp) dried oregano

1.5 litres (6 cups) chicken or vegetable stock (or water)

125 ml (½ cup) tomato purée

sea salt and a good sprinkling of sugar

2–3 bay leaves

60 g (a heaped ½ cup) small pasta shells

250 ml (1 cup) finely shredded spinach, or torn baby spinach leaves

1 x 410 g can borlotti beans, drained and rinsed

a small handful of fresh coriander leaves

baguettes or ciabatta, diagonally sliced

basil pesto

grated Parmesan cheese

Heat the oil in a large, deep saucepan and soften the onion. Add the garlic, celery, carrots, courgettes and oregano, and toss until just starting to soften and smell enticing. Add the stock, tomato purée, seasoning and bay leaves. Bring to the boil, then cover and simmer until the vegetables are soft – about 30 minutes. Add the pasta and spinach, and simmer for 10 minutes. Add the beans and coriander and heat through. Remove the bay leaves and check seasoning. Some time before the soup is ready, toast the bread on both sides and spread lightly with basil pesto. To serve, place a slice on the bottom of each (deep) soup bowl, ladle the soup over, and serve with Parmesan for sprinkling. **Serves 6.**

SIMPLE SEAFOOD SOUP
with arborio rice and pistou

The list of ingredients is quite long, but this is a really easy soup to make – the one essential being a good fish stock. This is much quicker to make than meat or poultry stocks, as it should be simmered for only 25–30 minutes before straining. As it's a chunky, filling soup, it can be served as a main course, followed by a salad and/or fresh fruit.

30 ml (2 Tbsp) olive oil and a pat of butter
1 large onion, finely chopped
1 large leek, finely sliced
2 medium carrots, finely diced
1 large stick celery, plus leaves, chopped
3 cloves garlic, crushed
1 x 5 cm strip lemon peel
2 bay leaves
75 ml (5 Tbsp) arborio rice (uncooked)
60 ml (¼ cup) white wine
1 x 410 g can peeled, diced tomatoes, plus juice
1 litre (4 cups) hot fish stock
sea salt and a little sugar to taste
400–450 g skinless white fish fillets, cubed
about 300 g mussels on the half-shell, thawed if frozen
a handful of chopped fresh flat-leaf parsley
basil pesto for topping

Heat the oil and butter in a large, deep saucepan. Soften the onion and leek, then add the carrots, celery, garlic, lemon peel, bay leaves, rice and wine. Toss for about 5 minutes to sweat and coat the rice, then add the tomatoes, stock and seasoning. Bring to the boil, then cover and simmer for about 30 minutes. Add the fish, mussels and parsley, and simmer, half-covered, just until the fish is cooked. Remove the bay leaves and lemon peel and check seasoning. Serve in deep bowls (not soup plates) with a small dollop of pesto (or pistou, seeing that it's in soup), a plate for the mussel shells, and plenty of bread for dipping. **Serves 4 generously.**

STARTERS
snacks, light meals and salads

smoked
SALMON SPREAD

120–160 g smoked salmon slices or offcuts

250 g smooth, low-fat cottage cheese

15 ml (1 Tbsp) fresh lemon juice

60 g very soft butter

a few drops of Tabasco sauce

5 ml (1 tsp) tomato paste (for colour)

a pinch each of sea salt and sugar (to taste)

milled black pepper

fresh dill to garnish

Place all the ingredients, except pepper and garnish, in a processor fitted with the metal blade and process until smooth. Check seasoning. Spoon into a glass container and refrigerate for a few hours. Spread thickly onto crustless, lightly buttered rye or wholewheat bread, grind a little pepper over, slice into fingers and serve garnished with fresh dill.
Makes 500 ml (2 cups).

smoked
SNOEK SPREAD

200 g smoked snoek

250 g smooth, low-fat cottage cheese

15 ml (1 Tbsp) fresh lemon juice

60 g very soft butter

30 ml (2 Tbsp) sweet chilli sauce

30 ml (2 Tbsp) finely snipped chives

paprika

Remove the skin from the snoek, slip out all the bones, then flake finely, feeling between your fingers to make sure you've got rid of them all. You should have 150 g. Put into a bowl with the rest of the ingredients, except the paprika. Mix well. Taste – it may need a pinch of salt and another 15 ml (1 Tbsp) chilli sauce. Spoon into a glass container, cover and refrigerate for several hours or overnight. Spread generously on crustless, lightly buttered wholewheat bread, dust with paprika and slice into fingers.
Makes about 500 ml (2 cups).

mushroom-cream
CHEESE SPREAD

15 ml (1 Tbsp) each oil and butter

60 ml (¼ cup) sherry

15 ml (1 Tbsp) soy sauce

5 ml (1 tsp) chopped fresh rosemary leaves

2 cloves garlic, crushed

1 small onion, finely chopped

250 g button mushrooms, wiped and finely chopped

250 g cream cheese (use low-fat if preferred)

60 ml (4 Tbsp) chopped fresh parsley

30 ml (2 Tbsp) snipped fresh chives

a pinch of sugar

Heat the oil, butter, sherry, soy sauce, rosemary, garlic and onion in a frying pan. Add the mushrooms and sauté until soft and the liquid has been absorbed (it should still be very moist). Remove from heat, stir in the cheese, then add the herbs and sugar. Taste to check seasoning, then spoon into a glass container, cover and refrigerate for at least a few hours to allow the flavours to blend. Serve on savoury biscuits.
Makes 500 ml (2 cups).

mushroom **CROSTINI**

Crisp bread rounds piled with a delectable, non-drip topping. The mushroom mixture may be made the day before and refrigerated, the bread cut and crisped hours in advance, and everything quickly baked when needed.

12–16 slices slightly stale bread

45 ml (3 Tbsp) oil and 20 ml (4 tsp) butter,
**   melted together**

extra 45 ml (3 Tbsp) butter

250 g button or brown mushrooms, wiped and
**   very finely chopped**

50 ml (3 Tbsp plus 1 tsp) flour

250 ml (1 cup) hot milk

6 spring onions, finely chopped

1 ml (¼ tsp) dried oregano

sea salt and milled black pepper

8 black olives, stoned and slivered

grated Parmesan or pecorino cheese

Slice the crusts off the bread and stamp out rounds using a 5–6 cm scone cutter (or use other shapes for variety). Place on a baking tray and brush both sides with the melted oil-butter mixture. Bake at 180 °C for 10–12 minutes, until crisp, turning once. Cool. Melt the extra butter in a saucepan, add the mushrooms and toss over low heat until all the liquid has evaporated. Sprinkle in the flour and, when absorbed, slowly add the milk. Bring to the boil and stir until very thick. Remove from heat and add the spring onions, oregano and seasoning to taste. (If working ahead, cool, cover and refrigerate.) To bake, spread the mushroom mixture thickly on each round of bread, top with olives and sprinkle with cheese. Bake at 200 °C for 12–15 minutes until piping hot. **Makes about 36.**

shrimp and cheese **CROSTINI**

The chunky topping can be mixed and refrigerated in advance. The bread rounds can also be pre-prepared. Assemble and grill just prior to serving.

white or plain brown bread, not too fresh
125 g cooked, peeled shrimps, coarsely chopped
125 ml (½ cup) grated gruyère or Cheddar cheese
2 spring onions, chopped
5 ml (1 tsp) Dijon mustard
45 ml (3 Tbsp) mayonnaise
2 ml (½ tsp) Worcestershire sauce
a little sea salt and milled black pepper

Using a 5 cm scone cutter, stamp out 12–14 circles from the bread and toast on one side only. Mix the remaining ingredients and spread on the untoasted side of each bread round. Arrange on a baking sheet, position well below the grill and grill until the cheese has melted. **Makes 12–14.**

TOMATO TARTLETS with olives, pesto and pecorino

A bit fiddly to prepare, but once you've got the bases made and tomatoes grilled you can line them up, stuff them and that's it. You need a small muffin tin, with the cups 5 cm in base diameter and 2 cm deep.

400 g ready-made puff pastry (defrost in the refrigerator)
12 bella tomatoes (these are the size of a very large acorn)
olive oil, sea salt, sugar and dried oregano
walnut pesto* (or pesto of choice)
12 black olives, stoned and quartered
pecorino cheese, finely grated
pine nuts

Roll out the pastry and cut out 12 circles, using a 7 cm cutter. Line the bases of the muffin cups with rounds of baking paper. Press a pastry circle into each, prick the bases several times, and bake at 200 °C for 15–20 minutes, or until risen, puffy and a light golden brown. Gently press down the centres to form a 'nest' and leave until cold before lifting out. You can do these in advance and store in a cake tin overnight.

For the filling, slice the tomatoes in half but not right through – open out, place cut sides up on a baking tray, sprinkle each with a few drops of olive oil, a pinch of salt, sugar and oregano, then grill until soft, juicy and beginning to shrivel. Nestle two halves in each pastry shell, top each with 2 ml (½ tsp) pesto and one quartered olive. Sprinkle with pecorino and gently press a few pine nuts into the top. Drizzle 2 ml (½ tsp) olive oil over each and place on a grill pan well below the griller, so that they will heat through gently without scorching. Remove when the nuts and pastry are lightly browned – be careful, they are soft and hot. Leave to cool a little before serving warm, or at room temperature. (They can be reheated.) **Makes 12.**

* WALNUT PESTO
Place the following in a processor fitted with the metal blade: 30 g each basil and flat-leaf parsley (rinsed and dried); 1 chopped clove garlic; and 8 walnut halves. Pulse finely and dribble in about 100 ml (⅖ cup) olive oil. Add a pinch of sea salt and 45 ml (3 Tbsp) finely grated pecorino cheese. Spoon into a jar, run a thin film of olive oil over the top and refrigerate.

MUSHROOM mountains

Delicious, assembled in minutes, and virtually everything can be done in advance. Best served as a starter as suggested, but if serving as a snack, use smaller mushrooms, a shorter baking time, and serve on crostini.

6 jumbo (400 g) brown mushrooms
fresh basil leaves
½ onion, coarsely grated
3 cloves garlic, crushed
firm but ripe tomatoes
sea salt and sugar
mozzarella cheese, sliced
dried oregano
olive oil
milled black pepper
rocket leaves

Slice the stems off the mushrooms and arrange the caps, hollows up, in a large, lightly oiled baking dish, then do the stuffing bit, one ingredient at a time, as follows: First a generous sprinkling of basil, then cover with onion, crush the garlic over, top with a thick slice of tomato, sprinkle the tomato (not the mushroom) with salt and sugar, cover with cheese, sprinkle with a few pinches of oregano, drizzle each mountain with 10–15 ml (2–3 tsp) olive oil and finish with a few grindings of black pepper. If working ahead, cover and refrigerate, but allow to return to room temperature before baking, uncovered, at 180 °C for about 30 minutes, until the mushrooms are soft and juicy, and the cheese has melted. Serve on a bed of rocket with the herbed French loaf.* **Serves 6**.

* BAKED FRENCH LOAF WITH FRESH HERB BUTTER
Mash together: 250 g soft butter; 125 ml (½ cup) chopped spring onions plus tops; a small handful of chopped parsley; 6 chopped sage leaves; 6 sprigs chopped marjoram leaves; 2 sprigs chopped thyme leaves; 2 cloves garlic, crushed (optional); a pinch of salt. Slice one large, long French loaf in 12 mm thick slices to the base, but not right through. Butter between the slices. If it oozes out at the top, scrape it off and slap it in again. Wrap in foil, leaving only the top exposed, and bake with the mushrooms for the last 15 minutes. **Enough for 30–40 slices**.

CUCUMBER CHEESECAKES with avocado

These make an unusual, minty, refreshing yet creamy hot-weather starter. Surround with salad leaves drizzled with a mustard vinaigrette* and serve with crispy rolls.

350 g English cucumber (that's 1 small or ½ large)
250 g smooth, low-fat cottage cheese (fat-free if preferred)
125 ml (½ cup) thick, low-fat Bulgarian yoghurt
2 ml (½ tsp) each sea salt and sugar
5 ml (1 tsp) Dijon mustard
22 ml (4½ tsp) gelatine
60 ml (¼ cup) cold water
30 ml (2 Tbsp) each finely chopped fresh parsley, chives and mint
125 ml (½ cup) thick cream, softly whipped
2 XL free-range egg whites, stiffly whisked
2 avocados, thinly segmented
milled black pepper for topping

Pare and grate the cucumber coarsely, and leave to drain in a colander – put a weight on top to squash out excess juice. Leave for 30 minutes then, using your hands, squeeze dry. You should have 250 ml (1 cup). Whisk together the cottage cheese, yoghurt, salt, sugar and mustard. Sponge the gelatine in the water and dissolve over simmering water. Slowly dribble it into the cheese mixture, whisking all the time. Stir in the cucumber and herbs, then fold in the cream and egg whites. Check seasoning, then pour into six ramekins (rinsed for easy unmoulding) – they should be wide in diameter so that once unmoulded there will be a flat surface for the avo. Refrigerate for several hours or overnight. Just before serving, arrange the avocado in overlapping circles to cover the tops, and dust with a few grinds of pepper. **Serves 6.**

* CREAMY MUSTARD VINAIGRETTE
Whizz the following in a blender: 2 spring onions plus a bit of the tops, chopped; 1 clove garlic, chopped; 30 ml (2 Tbsp) each white balsamic vinegar and fresh lemon juice; 250 ml (1 cup) olive oil; 10 ml (2 tsp) wholegrain mustard; a small handful of parsley tufts; 5 ml (1 tsp) runny honey; 5 ml (1 tsp) dried tarragon; a pinch of salt. Refrigerate in a glass jar and shake before using.

CHILLED SMOKED SALMON PATTIES with dilly mayo

These make the most elegant and enticing starters: plump little patties with a drizzle of light mayonnaise. Not too rich, not too expensive (the salmon is padded out with other things), not at all tricky to make, and everything tied up in advance – you can even make them a day ahead and refrigerate overnight. Present prettily on small plates.

160 g smoked salmon, finely snipped
(offcuts are fine to use)
1 hard-boiled free-range egg, chopped
4 slim spring onions, chopped
30 ml (2 Tbsp) finely chopped fresh parsley
5 ml (1 tsp) capers, rinsed and chopped
5 ml (1 tsp) Dijon mustard
10 ml (2 tsp) lime juice (or lemon, but use a little less)
200 g smooth, fat-free cottage cheese
milled black pepper and a little sea salt and
sugar to taste
extra salmon and dill to garnish (optional)

DILLY MAYO

30 ml (2 Tbsp) mayonnaise, preferably home-made
30 ml (2 Tbsp) thick plain yoghurt
10 ml (2 tsp) chopped fresh dill
2 ml (½ tsp) Dijon mustard
a small trickle of honey

For the salmon patties, mix everything together. To mould, you will need four to six small ramekins – flattish and shallow – 6 cm in diameter and 3 cm deep is just right. Four ramekins will give you really generous patties; six will provide small appetite-whetters – the better option if a good dinner is to follow. Line each with clingfilm, with enough overhang to cover the tops. Divide the mixture between the ramekins, pressing in gently to make a flat cake. Cover with the overhanging clingfilm and refrigerate for several hours or overnight. When needed, simply lift out of the ramekin, remove the clingfilm and out should plop a perfect patty. If garnishing, do so now.

For the mayonnaise, stir everything together until mixed, then cover and refrigerate. Makes just enough to spoon alongside or drizzle over 6 patties.

Serves 4–6.

brunch **MUESLI**

This nutritious muesli is a dry, untoasted mixture, and not a sweet and crunchy granola. Best of all, it should be put together a few hours in advance and refrigerated to soften and settle down. Please note that I have used the most convenient measures for the muesli mix, but you won't need it all – half is about enough, and the rest can be saved for tomorrow's breakfast.

MUESLI

2 x 250 ml (2 cups) oats

3 Weetbix biscuits, crushed – not too finely

100 ml (⅖ cup) sunflower seeds

125 ml (½ cup) seedless raisins

60 ml (4 Tbsp) wheatgerm

60 ml (4 Tbsp) desiccated coconut

fresh orange juice to moisten

FRUIT

750 g (prepared weight): use a selection of fresh fruit, including some juicy ones – cubed mangoes, sliced, ripe strawberries, diced bananas tossed in a little lemon juice – they're all good, but try to use lots of mango, because of its sweet juiciness

CREAMY YOGHURT

500 ml (2 cups) thick low-fat Bulgarian yoghurt

250 ml (1 cup) creamy Greek yoghurt

45 ml (3 Tbsp) runny honey

ground cinnamon for topping

Mix together all the ingredients for the muesli, except the orange juice. Toss the fruit together. Stir the yoghurts and honey until combined. Use a large serving dish with sides because the layers need to be spread out. First, spread one-third of the muesli mix to cover the base quite thickly. Drizzle with orange juice – just a little, for the oats to soak up in due course, else they will be too dry – but one doesn't want them mushy either. So, just a little juice. Then, a layer of half the fruit. Drizzle with half the yoghurt mixture. Repeat. Sprinkle the top quite generously with cinnamon, and refrigerate for about 2 hours – or more if convenient – before serving. **Serves 8–10.**

easy summer and winter **SMOOTHIES**

These are pure and really simple smoothies, just glowing with healthy vitamins. No artificial flavours or colourants or ice cream. Good anywhere, anytime, especially at a brunch. Ingredients easily stretched.

MANGO AND ORANGE SMOOTHIE

**1 jumbo or 2 medium sweet, ripe mangoes –
once skinned and pip discarded, the flesh
should weigh 350 g
125 ml (½ cup) fresh orange juice
30 ml (2 Tbsp) thick low-fat or full-cream
Bulgarian yoghurt
5 ml (1 tsp) honey or more to taste**

Place the mango pieces and orange juice in a blender and pulse until absolutely smooth. Add the yoghurt and honey, and blend again. Add more honey now if you like, but if the mango is ripe it should not be necessary. Serve immediately, or chill briefly. No garnish is necessary as it's a health drink, not a cocktail. Having said that, a sprig of mint will confirm the fresh, cool image.
These quantities make just less than 500 ml (2 cups), and certainly enough for 2 servings – and the variations are endless. Just blend what you like and what's in season – it's fun and very rewarding.

WINTER SMOOTHIE

**1 small, ripe papino or ½ small papaw,
weighing about 350 g
1 large banana, chopped
125 ml (½ cup) fresh orange juice
30 ml (2 Tbsp) plain low-fat or full-cream yoghurt
about 10 ml (2 tsp) runny honey (or to taste)**

Place all the ingredients in a blender and pulse until smooth. You could add ice to the glasses before pouring in these smoothies, but only a block or two so as not to dilute the fruity, vitamin-rich flavour.

savoury **DEEP EGGS**

Baked in ramekins, on a bed of freshly cooked tomatoes, bacon and corn, and topped with cheese, this makes a lovely change from scrambled eggs and omelettes. They're also more convenient as they don't need constant attention and are so easy to serve – one or two ramekins per person, with hot toast and butter. The size of the ramekins is important – 7 cm in diameter and 5 cm deep, but if you don't have them, use a shallow baking dish instead. Either way, these eggs are baked au bain-marie, *the ramekins standing in a larger pan/tin of simmering water. The quantities given are for four ramekins, but can easily be doubled or trebled.*

10 ml (2 tsp) each oil and butter
4 rashers lean, rindless back bacon (preferably unsmoked), diced
8 spring onions or slim baby leeks, chopped
400 g ripe, fresh tomatoes, skinned and chopped*
a few tufts of fresh parsley, chopped
sea salt, milled black pepper and a large pinch of sugar
80 ml (⅓ cup) cooked corn kernels
4 large or XL free-range eggs
grated Cheddar cheese and paprika for topping

Set the oven to 200 °C and at the same time put in the pan of water to heat up, so that it's ready to take the ramekins. Heat the oil and butter in a medium-sized frying pan and lightly sauté the bacon and onions or leeks. Add the tomatoes, parsley and seasoning and simmer, half-covered, for about 15 minutes until fairly thick; stir occasionally to mash up the tomatoes. If the mixture ends up looking watery, simply take off the lid and turn up the heat for a few minutes. Mix in the corn, check the seasoning, then spoon into the ramekins, dividing equally and levelly. Carefully break an egg on top of each, cover generously with cheese, dust with paprika, place in the pan/tin of hot water – the ramekins should not touch – and bake for about 20 minutes until the eggs are set and the cheese melted. Grab a fork and tuck in at once. **Serves 2–4.**

* Use sweet and rosy fresh tomatoes – canned won't do here.

EGG, CHEESE AND MUSHROOM bake

It's not quite a quiche, nor is it a tart, and it's not a frittata either, nor can you call it an omelette. But it's useful.
Served with grilled tomatoes and hot toast, this easy bake slots happily into the menu for a brunch or light lunch.

15 ml (1 Tbsp) oil
1 red pepper, seeded, ribs removed, and snipped
into small pieces
200 g button mushrooms, wiped and sliced
4 spring onions, plus some tops, chopped
5 ml (1 tsp) chopped fresh rosemary leaves
4 large free-range eggs
250 g smooth, low-fat cottage cheese
150 ml (⅗ cup) milk
45 ml (3 Tbsp) flour (absolutely level)
5 ml (1 tsp) mustard powder
a sprinkling of chopped fresh parsley
100 g mature Cheddar cheese, grated
sea salt and milled black pepper to taste
30 ml (2 Tbsp) dried, toasted breadcrumbs
for lining the pie dish
paprika for topping

Heat the oil and sauté the red pepper, mushrooms,
onions and rosemary until soft and aromatic; keep
the heat low and stir around for about 10 minutes, or
until the mixture is dry. Whisk together the eggs,
cottage cheese, milk, flour, mustard powder, parsley,
75 g of the Cheddar cheese, and the salt and
pepper, then stir it into the vegetable mixture.
Lightly oil a deep 23 cm pie dish. Sprinkle with the
breadcrumbs, swirl to coat and shake out the excess.
Pour in the egg mixture. Let it settle evenly, then
sprinkle with the remaining cheese and dust with
paprika. Bake at 160 °C for 30–35 minutes, or until
set. Leave to stand for a minute or two before slicing
into four large wedges. Remove with a spatula.
Serves 4.

TOASTED CHEESE special

This is a favourite savoury munch, almost as quick to make as ordinary cheese toast, but it looks much more appetising – all puffed up and golden brown on open slices of toast. Delicious served with coffee for a hearty elevenses snack, or even a quick lunch. Serve with knives and forks.

200 g Cheddar cheese, grated
2 ml (½ tsp) baking powder
2 XL free-range eggs, beaten
15 ml (1 Tbsp) wholegrain mustard
a little sea salt and milled black pepper
1 slim slice of onion, coarsely grated
20 ml (4 tsp) soft butter
wholewheat bread, sliced
2–3 tomatoes, thinly sliced
paprika for topping

Using a fork, mash the cheese, baking powder, eggs, mustard, seasoning, onion and butter together to make a coarse paste. Toast the bread on one side. Arrange a few slices of tomato on the untoasted side, and cover thickly with the cheese mixture. Dust with paprika, arrange on a heatproof platter and place under a hot grill – not too close, because the flavours have to come together, and there are eggs in there, and the cheese has to melt – but it takes only a few minutes to reach perfection. **Sufficient for 4–6 slices of bread, depending on size.**

ASPARAGUS with a choice of dressings

Buy the asparagus (slender and green, not thick and white) not more than one day in advance and keep refrigerated. Before poaching, rinse well and snap off the bases, then place in a single layer in a wide-based, shallow saucepan with a little lightly salted boiling water and cook briefly, uncovered, until tender-crisp. Refresh under cold water to set the colour, drain on paper towels and serve with dressing of choice.

QUICK MUSTARD MAYO

125 ml (½ cup) top-quality, off-the-shelf mayonnaise
125 ml (½ cup) low-fat Bulgarian yoghurt
15 ml (1 Tbsp) wholegrain mustard*
15 ml (1 Tbsp) pale, runny honey
1 ml (¼ tsp) dried tarragon, crushed

Gently mix all the ingredients with a spoon, turn into a glass jar, cover and refrigerate for a few hours.
Makes 250 ml

* Wholegrain mustards differ in density – you may want a little more.

ORANGE-MUSTARD MAYO

1 whole XL free-range egg plus 1 yolk*
50 ml (⅕ cup) fresh orange juice
2 ml (½ tsp) finely grated orange rind
a pinch of sea salt
10 ml (2 tsp) pale, runny honey
250 ml (1 cup) oil
15 ml (1 Tbsp) wholegrain mustard
5 ml (1 tsp) brandy

Place the egg and yolk, orange juice and rind, salt and honey in a blender and blend until thoroughly combined. Very slowly, while blending, dribble in the oil. When all the oil has been used, the mixture should have a medium-thick consistency. Stir in the mustard and brandy and refrigerate for several hours to thicken and to mature the flavour. **Serves 8–10.**

* Be very careful with uncooked egg yolks – keep the dressing refrigerated until the moment of serving, and if you wish to cut the richness of this dressing, gently fold in one part thick Bulgarian yoghurt to three parts dressing.

CREAMY YOGHURT SWIRLED WITH PESTO

And now for something completely different: Lightly 'marble' 250 ml (1 cup) Greek yoghurt with 15 ml (1 Tbsp) basil pesto – don't mix, leave it in streaks. Refrigerate until chilled, then spoon alongside or over the asparagus spears.

SALAD PLATTER
with blaauwkrantz and walnuts

... and roasted peppers, raw mushrooms and spinach, served with a whizzed blender dressing* and wholewheat rosemary and garlic ring bread (see page 196). It's a treat. And everything can be made in the blink of an eye.

250 g button mushrooms, just the very tips of the stems removed, then wiped and thinly sliced

60 ml (¼ cup) oil

30 ml (2 Tbsp) fresh lemon juice

1 clove garlic, crushed

2 red peppers, halved, seeds and ribs removed, flattened, then grilled, skinned and sliced into strips

4–6 spring onions, chopped, or chopped, blanched baby leeks

150 g mixed salad leaves (baby spinach, butter lettuce, etc.)

a little sea salt

100 g Blaauwkrantz cheese, crumbled

40–50 g walnuts, toasted and chopped (a light toasting or roasting really makes a difference to the flavour)

Place the prepared mushrooms in a large glass bowl. (No salt at this stage.) Immediately toss with the oil, lemon juice and garlic. Mix in the red peppers and spring onions, cover and set aside or chill for up to 3 hours if working ahead. When ready to plate, line a large platter with the salad leaves. Spoon the mushroom mixture over evenly, salt lightly, then sprinkle with the cheese and walnuts. **Serves 4.**

* BLENDER DRESSING

250 ml (1 cup) oil

60 ml (¼ cup) white balsamic vinegar (or half vinegar, half lemon juice)

a few tufts of fresh parsley and celery leaves

5 ml (1 tsp) mustard powder

5 ml (1 tsp) Worcestershire sauce

10 ml (2 tsp) honey

a pinch of sea salt

Whizz all the ingredients together, pour into a decanter, and pass for diners to help themselves, along with the beautiful ring loaf and butter.

LAYERED TUNA,
bean and egg salad

An unsophisticated salad, effortless, quickly put together, and a complete meal. Serve with hot Italian rolls, instant herbed oil* for dipping, and salad leaves with rocket.

600 g ripe but firm tomatoes, sliced
a sprinkling of sugar
sea salt and milled black pepper
1 bunch spring onions, chopped
a small handful of fresh basil leaves, roughly torn
2 x 410 g cans cannellini beans, rinsed, drained and patted dry
2 x 150 or 170 g cans shredded tuna or tuna chunks in oil*
15–30 ml (1–2 Tbsp) balsamic vinegar
45 ml (3 Tbsp) cold-pressed, extra virgin olive oil
4 hard-boiled eggs, sliced
chopped fresh flat-leaf parsley

Layer the ingredients in the given order (that is, starting with the tomatoes and carrying straight on) on a large platter with slightly raised sides. Make just one layer of each ingredient, spreading evenly, or drizzling when using the vinegar and oil. Cover loosely and leave to stand for about 30 minutes before serving. **Serves 4 generously.**

* Tuna in water can be used, if preferred, but drain it well; or use one can in oil, and one can in water, and adjust the quantity of olive oil accordingly.

* INSTANT HERBED OIL

Pour 150 ml (⅗ cup) olive oil, and the same of canola or sunflower oil, into a small, deep, heavy-based saucepan, add 2 sprigs fresh rosemary and 4 sprigs fresh thyme (about 10 cm each); 2 crumbled bay leaves; 2 fresh sage leaves, bruised; and 2 cloves garlic, peeled and slightly smashed. Stir to moisten, then heat slowly until just popping, not boiling. Leave to pop very gently for 6–8 minutes, giving the occasional stir to bruise the herbs, until it is blissfully aromatic. Remove from the stove, leave it to stop hissing and cool down, then strain. Once cooled, pour into a decanter and pass for individual drizzling.

SMOKED SALMON luncheon salad

Diners frequently sit and look at this for some time before tucking in. The colour-combination is just brilliant: creamy salmon, avocado, beetroot and rocket – and yet this flamboyant salad is dead easy to prepare. All you have to cook is the beetroot. Once that's over with, and the salmon mixture mixed, it's simply a matter of arranging the ingredients attractively, either on one large platter or on single-serving plates, along with sliced rye bread and butter. Fabulous.

1 bunch (600–700 g) small to medium beetroot
2 x 250 g tubs plain smooth low-fat cottage cheese,
  drained if necessary
200–250 g smoked salmon, snipped (offcuts are fine)
125 ml (½ cup) cultured sour cream
finely grated rind of ½ small lemon
6–8 slim spring onions, plus some tops, finely chopped
5 ml (1 tsp) Dijon mustard
a few drops of Tabasco sauce
about 60 g rocket and a pillow-pack of salad leaves,
  mixed
3–4 avocados
milled black pepper and chopped walnuts for topping

Scrub the beetroot gently so as not to break the skin and cut off the tops (leave on 2 cm), then boil or roast – the latter is tastier, but takes longer. Cool, then skin and pat dry. Meanwhile, combine the cottage cheese, salmon, sour cream, lemon rind, onions, mustard and Tabasco. Refrigerate in a covered glass bowl for a few hours for the flavours to develop. Just before serving, slice the beetroot thinly and arrange on the platter. Next, make a circle of rocket and salad leaves. Then come the slices of avocado. The salmon mixture goes in the centre – pile it into one or more nice little bowls to make it easier to dip into. Top with freshly milled pepper and a good sprinkling of walnuts. (If the platter is too full already, put the bowl of salmon alongside.) If serving on one large platter, add a fork for spearing and a spoon for the salmon dip. **Serves 6.**

summer **SALAD PLATTER**

A brilliant salad that can be served either as a starter or as a main course if you double up on the ingredients. Use a really large platter and the vegetables almost dictate the arrangement themselves – salad leaves around the edge, wedges of feta in between, the roasted veg in the centre, the anchovies and olives patterning the top. The basil oil* goes into a jug for sprinkling, and a crusty loaf goes somewhere.

2 aubergines (brinjals) (total 300 g), washed, halved and sliced into short fingers

200 g large brown mushrooms, halved

2 medium red peppers, seeded, ribs removed, and cut into strips

8 pickling onions, peeled and halved vertically

30 ml (2 Tbsp) each olive oil and water

2 cloves garlic, crushed

2 ml (½ tsp) each dried oregano and sea salt

2 sprigs of fresh rosemary

200 g tomatoes, sliced into quarters and diced

mixed salad leaves and baby spinach, perhaps rocket if you have it

feta cheese, sliced into fingers

1 x 40 g can anchovied sardines, briefly soaked in milk

black olives

Place the aubergine fingers in a colander, sprinkle with salt, and leave for 30 minutes. Rinse and dry well. Arrange the aubergines, mushrooms, red peppers and onions in a large baking dish. Mix the oil, water, garlic, oregano and salt together; mix into the vegetables and tuck in the rosemary. Roast at 200 °C for 30 minutes, or until the aubergine is cooked. Remove from the oven, mix in the fresh tomatoes, discard the rosemary, then cool. Plate as suggested above or try your own arrangement, then stand back and look, and be very proud. **Serves about 4.**

* BASIL OIL

Whizz the following in a blender: a handful of fresh basil leaves; 125 ml (½ cup) olive oil; 60 ml (¼ cup) water; 10 ml (2 tsp) lemon juice; a pinch each of sea salt and sugar. It's difficult to estimate servings, but if you have more than four diners, it's best to double up.

SMOKED SALMON
and green bean salad

Because smoked salmon is expensive, it's a good idea to pad it out to make it go further. In the following starter salad the addition of anchovies and slim-as-a-bridge-pencil green beans do the trick, and the result is an unusual combination, topped with a skein of salmon and served with lightly buttered rye bread. Nevertheless, it is a special-occasion and not a budget salad.

400 g very slim green beans, trimmed and halved diagonally OR 300 g green beans and 200 g button mushrooms, wiped and thinly sliced
1 large onion, sliced into thin rings
2 ml (½ tsp) dried dill
1 large red or yellow pepper, seeded, ribs removed, and julienned
120–160 g thin slices of smoked salmon
sour cream, milled black pepper and lemon slices to garnish

DRESSING
100 ml (⅖ cup) oil
1 x 50 g can anchovy fillets, drained and briefly soaked in milk, then drained again
a few tufts of fresh parsley
30 ml (2 Tbsp) fresh lemon juice
a pinch of sugar

Cook the beans, mushrooms (if using), onion and dill in a little unsalted water in a large frying pan until the beans are tender and still bright green – don't cover the pan completely, keep the lid tilted. While this is happening, make the dressing by placing the oil, half the anchovies and the rest of the ingredients in a blender and blend until smooth. When the beans are ready, drain (but do not refresh), place in a bowl, pour the dressing over, fork in the red or yellow pepper, cool, then cover and chill for 3–4 hours. Just before serving, toss in the remaining anchovies, chopped, and arrange on individual small plates. Top with the salmon, a dollop of sour cream, and a dusting of pepper, and place a slice of lemon on the side. Serve with rye bread. **Makes 6 small servings.**

ROSEMARY PEAR SALAD
and blue cheese dressing

A combination of layers of leafy greens, roasted peppers, walnuts and subtly perfumed pears, this salad looks lovely piled onto a large, shallow platter to show off the ingredients and colours before they all get mixed up. Easy to prepare in advance, and the quantities for leafy ingredients are adaptable; the pears will slot into a salad for four to six, so double up for a jumbo salad; the dressing, served separately, will do for about ten servings.

BASE SALAD

A mixture of baby spinach, rocket, watercress and lettuce leaves.

PEPPERS

2 large red peppers, halved, seeds and ribs removed, opened out flat and grilled until blistered and blackened. Cover with a damp towel, remove skin and slice into strips.

PEARS

Peel and halve 3 large, not-quite-ripe pears. Place in a wide pan, rounded sides up, sprinkle each half with a pinch of sugar and 5 ml (1 tsp) fresh lemon juice, add 250 ml (1 cup) water and 2 x 10 cm sprigs rosemary, bring to the boil, then reduce the heat and simmer, covered, until just tender. Leave to cool, uncovered, then remove the pears and refrigerate. Before serving, remove pips and cores and slice.

TOPPING

Coarsely chopped walnuts or pecan nuts.

DRESSING

Place in a blender and blend until creamy: 250 ml (1 cup) oil (half olive, half canola or sunflower); 90 ml (6 Tbsp) fresh lemon juice; 60 g blue cheese, crumbled (or more to taste); 5 ml (1 tsp) Worcestershire sauce; 1 small clove garlic, chopped; a few tufts of fresh parsley; 2 spring onions, chopped; a trickle of honey. Pour into a jug, refrigerate, and shake or whisk just before serving. For a milder, creamier dressing, stir in up to 125 ml (½ cup) thick plain yoghurt.

ACCOMPANIMENT

Baguette slices, brushed with olive oil, toasted and rubbed with a cut clove of garlic.

NUTTY COUSCOUS SALAD with spices and preserved lemons

A couscous salad that combines a succulent stir-fry with fresh coriander, walnuts and a lemony surprise simply has to be special. For a sparkling addition to a cold buffet, serve it on a beautiful platter – use a large one because the quantities are generous.

125 ml (½ cup) olive oil

a large nut of butter

2 bunches spring onions, chopped

1 large red pepper, seeded, ribs removed, and diced

250 g brown mushrooms, wiped and finely chopped*

5 ml (1 tsp) each ground cinnamon and cumin

10 ml (2 tsp) ground coriander

80–100 g walnuts, chopped

sea salt and milled black pepper to taste

a generous squeeze of fresh lemon juice

500 ml (2 cups) quick-cooking couscous

5 ml (1 tsp) turmeric

2 medium preserved lemons, rinsed, flesh removed and
   discarded, and the rind snipped into small pieces –
   about 60 ml (4 Tbsp) altogether

fresh coriander and extra walnuts to garnish

Gently heat the oil and butter, add the onions and red pepper and sauté briefly. Add the mushrooms and keep tossing; when they start to shrink, sprinkle in the cinnamon, cumin and ground coriander. Toss for a few more seconds until you get the aroma, then remove the pan from the stove, mix in the walnuts, seasoning and lemon juice, then cover loosely and set aside.

Prepare the couscous – follow instructions on the box, adding the turmeric to the water. When done and swollen, tip into a large bowl and fork in the vegetable and nut mixture, adding any juices left in the pan. Add the preserved lemon. Mix lightly until well combined but not clumpy, then turn into a salad bowl to cool for 1–2 hours, loosely covered. To gloss it before serving, fork in a splosh of olive oil, then garnish. If working ahead, refrigerate (once cooled) in a covered glass bowl (without the garnish) for a few hours, but expect to lose a little of the flavour. **Serves about 10.**

* Brown mushrooms do darken the mixture, but are preferable to button mushrooms because they have so much more flavour.

CURRIED STAMPKORING salad

Stampkoring is a nutty grain with homespun appeal. It takes longer to cook than rice, but the following method cuts down on time. Serve at any cold buffet, barbecue, or summer lunch with things on the side, like green leaves and avocado, yoghurt, hard-boiled eggs and chutney.

250 ml (1 cup) stampkoring (pearled whole wheat)

700 ml (2⅘ cups) water

2 ml (½ tsp) turmeric

5 ml (1 tsp) sea salt and a dash of oil

60 ml (¼ cup) oil

1 large onion, sliced into thin rings

½ red pepper, seeded, ribs removed, and diced

2 cloves garlic, crushed

3 courgettes (baby marrows) (150 g), pared and very finely diced

15 ml (1 Tbsp) curry powder

5 ml (1 tsp) ground cumin

2 ml (½ tsp) ground coriander

60 ml (4 Tbsp) seedless raisins

30 ml (2 Tbsp) chopped fresh coriander leaves and stems

60 ml (4 Tbsp) sunflower seeds

Rinse the stampkoring and soak, generously covered with cold water, for at least 2 hours. Bring the 700 ml (2⅘ cups) water to the boil in a deep saucepan, adding the turmeric, salt and dash of oil. Drain the stampkoring, tip into the boiling water, stir, and reduce the heat to very low. Simmer, covered, for 45 minutes, until the water is absorbed and the grains are soft. (Once ready, it will burn, so keep an eye on it.) Meanwhile, heat the 60 ml (¼ cup) oil in a large frying pan and add the onion, red pepper, garlic and courgettes. Toss until softening and glistening, then add all the spices and the raisins. Stir briefly over low heat until aromatic. If the stampkoring isn't ready, cover the frying pan and set aside for a while. Tip the cooked stampkoring into a large bowl and immediately fork in the hot, spicy vegetables in oil. Add the fresh coriander and the sunflower seeds, check for salt and perhaps a little lemon juice, then set aside and, when it stops steaming, cover loosely. Serve at room temperature. The salad may also be refrigerated overnight, in a covered glass bowl.

Serves 4–8.

LEAFY GREEN SALAD
with asparagus and pesto dressing

There was a time when a side salad meant lettuce, raw onion and chopped tomato sitting there in a bowl, as boring as could be, idly picked at and eventually binned. And yet it is so easy – and so important – to add a bit of interest to a salad. It has become an integral part of a meal – after all, we should all be eating something raw with our mains every day. This one is best served with something grilled as it's an oil-rich salad, but it's a good, lusciously green combination.*

250 g fresh asparagus cuts**
250 g mixed green salad leaves (try to include baby spinach and rocket)
1 bunch spring onions, chopped
sliced avocado and a small sprinkling of toasted pine nuts for topping***

DRESSING
100–125 ml (⅖ –½ cup) olive oil
30 ml (2 Tbsp) basil pesto
45 ml (3 Tbsp) fresh lemon juice
5 ml (1 tsp) runny honey

Boil the asparagus in a little lightly salted water for a few minutes until cooked but not *pap* – keep the lid of the saucepan slightly tilted to help retain the bright colour. Drain, then refresh under the cold tap and gently pat dry. If working ahead, refrigerate.

Make the dressing by whisking all the ingredients together. Mix the leaves, onions and asparagus in a salad bowl, pour the dressing over, toss gently to mix, then garnish with the avo and a sprinkling of nuts. **Serves 6.**

* If it's all just too green, add a spot of colour by sprinkling a red salad pepper, cut into small dice, on the top before adding the avo.
** Asparagus cuts are sold ready-cut into smallish pieces and are inexpensive. If you can't find them, try substituting slim, julienned green beans.
*** Pine nuts are a delicious indulgence. Pecans can be substituted but the composition won't be the same.

POTATO AND CORN SALAD
with mustard dressing

Gone are the days of the old-fashioned version of waxy potato salad floating in cooked salad cream. This one is much more interesting and very good with ham.

750–800 g medium new potatoes, scrubbed and cubed*
5 ml (1 tsp) dried tarragon
45 ml (3 Tbsp) vinaigrette (mix half olive oil, half lemon juice, and crushed garlic)
375 ml (1½ cups) cooked corn kernels, well drained**
1 bunch spring onions, chopped
125 ml (½ cup) thick mayonnaise
125 ml (½ cup) Greek or thick low-fat Bulgarian yoghurt
30 ml (2 Tbsp) wholegrain mustard
10 ml (2 tsp) Dijon mustard
a little runny honey to taste
fresh tarragon if possible, otherwise chopped fresh parsley to garnish

Boil the cubed potatoes in a little salted water, with the dried tarragon. Drain, shake dry and turn into a shallow, but wide-based salad bowl. Pour the vinaigrette over while the potatoes are still warm and shake gently to coat the cubes evenly. Gently mix in the corn and onions, and leave until cold and the dressing has been absorbed. Meanwhile, stir together the remaining ingredients, except the garnish, until smooth, and pour half over the salad. Leave for about 10 minutes and, if you think it needs more (so much depends on the shape of your dish), drizzle over a little extra, then garnish and serve. Best freshly made, but this is not always convenient, in which case cover the cooled salad and refrigerate, as well as the remaining dressing, then add another trickle just before serving if the salad has absorbed too much while chilling. **Serves 6.**

* Be sure to use firm, white potatoes and not waxy or baking potatoes.
** Frozen corn is the most convenient to use, but if you're desperate for time, a can will do – rinse and drain very well and bear in mind that the kernels will probably be sugared if canned.

lemony green bean, pepper and
MUSHROOM SALAD

This bright, crunchy salad goes with anything – fish, lamb, chicken, or tossed into cooked, cooled pasta and served as a main dish. This is possibly my favourite, topped with feta or pecorino. The cheerful colours are a bonus and it does not need a garnish.

75 ml (5 Tbsp) olive oil

1 large onion, sliced into thin rings and separated

1 red pepper, seeded, ribs removed, and julienned

1 yellow pepper, seeded, ribs removed, and julienned

250 g button mushrooms, wiped and quartered

2–3 cloves garlic, crushed

300 g slender green beans, topped, tailed and
   sliced diagonally, or left whole if pencil thin

45 ml (3 Tbsp) soy sauce (preferably low-salt)

30 ml (2 Tbsp) fresh lemon juice

5 ml (1 tsp) very finely grated lemon rind

60 ml (¼ cup) water

7–10 ml (1½–2 tsp) runny honey

Heat the oil in a large frying pan. Add the onion, allow to soften and turn yellow, then add the peppers, mushrooms and garlic. Stir-fry until just tender, then use a slotted spoon to transfer everything to a large, flattish salad bowl. To the pan add the remaining ingredients. Stir to mix, then cover and cook over low heat until the beans are just tender-crisp. Tip into the bowl with the first lot of ingredients, adding any juices from the pan. Toss everything together until glossy and glistening, and leave until no longer steaming before covering loosely and leaving to stand for at least 1 hour (to allow the full flavour to develop) before serving.
Serves 6 modestly.

cinnamon-roasted
BUTTERNUT SALAD

If I were to spell out the entire title it would run on to two full lines or more, and I know that recipes with more than seven words in the title tend to frighten people. But I have to say that this salad also contains red and yellow peppers, olives, feta cheese, basil and balsamic vinegar, and yet it is really straightforward to prepare and looks like a picture in a dish. Perfect with pasta or lamb, or centred at a buffet, which is where I first met this technicolour beauty and was prompted to devise my own version.

2 large red and 2 large yellow peppers, halved, seeded and ribs removed
1 large butternut, peeled, seeds and stringy bits discarded, cubed (1.2 kg prepared weight)
60 ml (¼ cup) olive oil
30 ml (2 Tbsp) light brown sugar
5 ml (1 tsp) ground cinnamon and a little sea salt
crumbled feta cheese
stoned black olives
a few fresh basil leaves, torn
20 ml (4 tsp) balsamic vinegar

Flatten the peppers and place spread out on a grill pan. Grill until blackened. Remove, wrap in a damp tea towel and set aside while you switch off the griller, turn up the oven heat to 220 °C, and attend to the butternut. Spread the cubes in a single layer on a large baking sheet lined with baking paper. Drizzle the olive oil over as evenly as you can, then sprinkle with the sugar, cinnamon and salt. Roast for about 20 minutes, until browned and soft. Skin the peppers, slice into thin strips, add to the butternut and turn everything into a large, flattish salad bowl. Leave to cool, then sprinkle with the feta, olives and basil and finally drizzle with the vinegar to cut the sweetness. If working ahead, cover the butternut-pepper mixture loosely once it has stopped steaming, then add the remaining ingredients just before serving. **Serves 8.**

FISH
and seafood

FISH WITH LIME-CHIVE BUTTER
and glazed mushrooms

Kabeljou (kob), with its firm, succulent flesh, is the perfect choice for this recipe. Fish often responds best when fiddled with least, and this is a fine example of just how good it can be when given the easy, no-fuss treatment. The mushrooms make a fabulous (also dead easy) accompaniment.

1 smallish lime
60 g soft butter
30 ml (2 Tbsp) finely snipped fresh chives
a dash of Pernod (optional)
4 large (about 700 g), skinless fish fillets, preferably kabeljou
oil and sea salt

Start by making the butter. Use a zester or a coarse grater for the lime, and then chop the peel finely, or snip with a pair of kitchen scissors. Reserve the shaved lime to use for juice later on. Mix the peel with the butter, chives and Pernod, if using. Roll into a long sausage, wrap in greaseproof paper and refrigerate until firm.

Shortly before you want to eat, line a shallow baking dish with greaseproof paper and brush with oil. Place the fish fillets on the paper, brush the tops very lightly with oil, sprinkle with salt and drizzle with lime juice. Bake at 180 °C until cooked through – the time depends on the thickness of the fish – probably 25 minutes.

While the fish is baking, slice the butter into coins and, just before serving, place one or two coins on top of each fillet. Return to the oven until they just start to melt and spread, then serve, using a spatula to lift out onto serving plates. **Serves 4.**

GLAZED MUSHROOMS
These little nuggets can be prepared in advance, spooned into a baking dish, and reheated in the oven shortly before the fish is done.

250 g button mushrooms
45 ml (3 Tbsp) medium-sweet sherry
45 ml (3 Tbsp) chicken stock
15 ml (1 Tbsp) soy sauce
10 ml (2 tsp) tomato paste
5 ml (1 tsp) treacle sugar
a little chopped fresh parsley

Wipe the mushrooms with damp kitchen paper and, if large, slice into halves or quarters. Place in a wide-based frying pan in a single layer. Mix the sherry, stock, soy sauce and tomato paste together and pour over the mushrooms, then sprinkle with the sugar. Bring to the boil and cook over high heat, tossing and stirring. The mushrooms will release a lot of liquid at first, but as the liquid reduces they will start to sizzle in their own juices – watch for burning. Remove from the heat as soon as the liquid evaporates into caramelly bubbles. Spoon into a shallow baking dish, rinse out the frying pan with just a dash of water, drizzle over the mushrooms to keep them moist, sprinkle with parsley and reheat briefly, as suggested above.

spicy **FISH CURRY**

This is a really simple, basic, non-gourmet curry.
There's no seafood in here, only hake – and frozen at that –
so plebeian it is, but it's useful and economical and the end result
is a jolly tasty dish with a bright, tangy sauce.

45 ml (3 Tbsp) olive oil

1 medium onion, finely chopped

1–2 red chillies, seeded and chopped

2–3 cloves garlic, crushed

20 ml (4 tsp) curry powder

5 ml (1 tsp) ground cumin

2 ml (½ tsp) ground fennel

1 x 425 g can chopped tomatoes in juice

125 ml (½ cup) fish or chicken stock

30 ml (2 Tbsp) smooth chutney

2 bay leaves

5 ml (1 tsp) tomato paste

a little sugar

500 g skinned and filleted frozen hake portions
   (hake steaks are convenient)

seasoned flour

fresh coriander leaves

Heat the oil gently in a large frying pan, add the
onion, chillies and garlic and, when softening, add
the spices, stirring for a few seconds over low heat.
Add the tomatoes, stock, chutney, bay leaves, tomato
paste and a sprinkling of sugar to offset the tartness
of the canned tomatoes. Stir to mix, then, when the
liquid begins to pop, cover and simmer very gently
for about 20 minutes to concentrate the flavour. Dust
the fish lightly with the seasoned flour, shaking off
any excess, and slide into the sauce. Keeping the
heat low, cover and simmer until the fish is cooked
right through – turn once and add a little extra stock
or white wine if the sauce has thickened too much.
Cooking time depends on the size of your pan and
the thickness of the fillets. When done, remove the
bay leaves, and sprinkle with lots of fresh coriander.
Serves 4.

PILAFF WITH MUSHROOMS and garlic prawns

A pilaff can be a simple side dish of rice cooked in stock, or fattened up as a main dish by adding meat, veg or poultry. This recipe features prawns, and because they don't come cheap, the pilaff is padded out with mushrooms and tomatoes, with the garlicky, buttery prawns and a crumble of feta coming in at the end. The result, in about 30 minutes flat, is a pink, succulent pilaff ready to be ladled into deep bowls for individual servings.

150 ml (⅗ cup) tomato purée

300 ml (1⅕ cups) fish stock (chicken is second best)

30 ml (2 Tbsp) olive oil

1 medium onion, finely chopped

250 g button mushrooms, wiped and sliced

250 ml (1 cup) uncooked long-grain white rice,
rinsed and drained

2 medium tomatoes, skinned and chopped

60 ml (¼ cup) white wine

2 bay leaves

5 ml (1 tsp) each sea salt and sugar

15 ml (1 Tbsp) olive oil

30 ml (2 Tbsp) butter

300 g (or more) shelled, deveined, defrosted prawns

3–4 cloves garlic, crushed

a squeeze of fresh lemon juice

90–100 g feta cheese, cubed

a few fresh basil leaves, torn

a few fried or grilled prawn tails to garnish (optional)

Heat the tomato purée with the stock, then set aside. Heat the oil in a deep, wide saucepan, and add the onion and mushrooms. Toss over a low heat until softening, then add the rice. Stir until coated, then add the hot liquid, tomatoes, wine, bay leaves, salt and sugar. Bring to the boil, then cover and simmer over very low heat until the rice is tender and the liquid absorbed – 25 minutes. Heat the second quantity of oil and butter in a frying pan and add the prawns (if using a larger quantity of prawns, add a little extra butter/oil). Toss until pink, curled, opaque and cooked through – this does not take long. Towards the end of the cooking time, crush in the garlic, and sprinkle in the lemon juice. Tip the whole lot into the cooked pilaff, and fork in the feta and basil. Remove from heat, cover, and leave to stand for 5 minutes. Remove the bay leaves, check seasoning, and serve.

Serves 4–5.

CALAMARI on shells

Serve this silky calamari on pasta shells. It isn't quite a soup, nor a sauce, but a sort of rich broth with a waft of tangy gremolata*. The slow simmer, acid tomatoes and wine will tenderize the calamari beautifully. Add a basket of crusty rolls, and follow with a salad for a lovely, lusty meal.

1 kg cleaned calamari tubes

1 x 410 g can chopped tomatoes

60 ml (¼ cup) dry white wine

10 ml (2 tsp) tomato paste

10 ml (2 tsp) soft brown sugar

2 ml (½ tsp) each paprika, dried oregano and sea salt

30 ml (2 Tbsp) olive oil

1 large onion, finely chopped

125 ml (½ cup) fish or chicken stock

3 bay leaves

15 ml (1 Tbsp) soft butter

15 ml (1 Tbsp) flour

250 g small pasta shells

Slit the calamari tubes down one side, open out flat, remove any spiny bits that might have been left behind, then cut across into thin strips. Dry as thoroughly as possible. Whizz the tomatoes, wine, tomato paste, sugar, paprika, oregano and salt in a blender. Heat the oil in a deep, wide saucepan. Add the onion and, when golden, add the calamari. Keep tossing just until the calamari stiffens and turns white, then reduce the heat immediately, pour over the blended tomato sauce and the fish stock, and slip in the bay leaves. Simmer over very low heat, stirring occasionally and keeping the lid of the saucepan tilted, for about 1 hour, by which time the calamari should be very tender and the sauce mellow and plentiful. To thicken it for coating the pasta, mash the butter and flour to a paste and stir small pats into the sauce, then sprinkle with the gremolata. Heat for a few minutes, uncovered, to mingle all the flavours, then ladle into the bowls over the cooked pasta. **Serves 4.**

* GREMOLATA

Mix a handful of chopped flat-leaf parsley with a crushed clove of garlic and the finely grated rind of ½ lemon.

SALMON with stir-fried vegetables

If you dislike frying fish, try this one. It's a super, stove-top dish, delicately touched with Oriental seasonings
that don't intrude on the fine flavour of Cape salmon, but it's also good with the old faithful – hake.
The one imperative: a very large pan – 28 x 6 cm is perfect.

45 ml (3 Tbsp) oil
5 ml (1 tsp) dark sesame oil
a bunch of spring onions or a few baby leeks, chopped
a small knob of fresh root ginger, peeled and
coarsely grated
3 medium carrots, julienned
180 g slender green beans, trimmed and
diagonally sliced
½ English cucumber (250 g), pared and julienned
(seeds discarded)
125 g button mushrooms, wiped and sliced
4 Cape salmon fillets (550–600 g total weight),
skin removed
sea salt and milled black pepper
toasted almond flakes to garnish

SAUCE
250 ml (1 cup) fish or chicken stock
30 ml (2 Tbsp) cornflour
about 30 ml (2 Tbsp) soy sauce
5 ml (1 tsp) honey
2–5 ml (½–1 tsp) finely grated lemon rind

Heat the oils in that large pan and stir-fry the spring onions or leeks, ginger, carrots and beans until softening but still crunchy. (You could also cover the pan and let them steam over a low heat.) Add the cucumber and mushrooms, and toss until wilting. Stir together all the ingredients for the sauce, add to the pan and, when bubbling and thickened, reduce the heat to very low and arrange the lightly seasoned fish on top of the vegetables. Cover and allow to simmer very gently for 10–12 minutes, or until the fish is just cooked through. Using a slotted spoon, carefully transfer the fillets to a warmed serving platter, best side up, sprinkle with almonds and spoon the saucy vegetables alongside. **Serves 4**.

ROASTED FISH,
Italian-style

I've never eaten this dish in Italy and possibly the Italians haven't either, but it's as good a name as any for fish teamed up with Mediterranean ingredients. It's a favourite, this one, rating tops for simplicity and flavour. Only a few special ingredients are required, but they are important to ensure that the dish ends up as it should – succulent, flavoursome, and so satisfying that you don't need pasta or potatoes or anything but a green salad to accompany it.

4 kabeljou (kob) fillets (about 180 g each, preferably the long, tail-end fillets)
fresh lemon juice
300 g bella (or baby plum) tomatoes, halved
6 spring onions, plus some tops, chopped
5 ml (1 tsp) Italian Herb Seasoning (mixed dried herbs)
200 g portabellini mushrooms, wiped and quartered
sea salt
60 ml (¼ cup) olive oil
60 ml (¼ cup) off-dry white wine
finely grated pecorino cheese and pine nuts for topping

Arrange the fillets, skin side down, in a large baking dish or roaster, base lined with baking paper. Be sure to leave plenty of room round the sides for the vegetables. Sprinkle the fish with a little lemon juice. Toss together the tomatoes, spring onions, dried herbs and mushrooms and, when well mixed, scatter all round the fish – not on top. Sprinkle everything with salt, then mix the oil and wine and pour that over everything. Sprinkle the fish with a little of the cheese, and then with pine nuts – just 5 ml (1 tsp) per fillet will do. Now roast, uncovered, just below the centre of the oven at 200 °C for about 25 minutes, until the fish is cooked through and the tomatoes and mushrooms have started to shrivel and release their juices. Serve right away. **Serves 4.**

ROASTED CAPE SALMON
with butter and herbs

An amazingly effortless fish dish – no frying, no turning, no grilling, no garnishing. It's astonishing that it can turn out so well when almost all that is required of the cook is the making of the butter – that, and having in hand a perfect piece of thick, skinned salmon fillet weighing 500 g. The dill and tarragon used in this recipe are dried, because all too often they are unobtainable fresh – either they're out of season, or the supermarket is fresh out. But dried herbs, freshly bought, make an excellent butter, and the flavour of this dish is lovely.

60 g soft butter
1 ml (¼ tsp) dried dill
1 ml (¼ tsp) dried tarragon
15 ml (1 Tbsp) finely snipped fresh chives
15 ml (1 Tbsp) finely chopped fresh parsley
2 ml (½ tsp) finely grated lemon rind
500 g skinless salmon fillet in one piece of even thickness
60 ml (¼ cup) white wine (Sauvignon Blanc is good)
sea salt

First cream the butter with the herbs and lemon rind, mixing well. Roll into a sausage shape, wrap and refrigerate for about 1 hour, or until firm enough to slice. To bake, place the fish in a baking dish – not a big one – it should fit fairly snugly with a bit of room to spare for the juices. Pour the wine in at the side and season the fish lightly. Slice the butter into six coins and place them on top of the fish. Roast at 200 °C for 15 minutes, then remove from the oven and spread any blobs of butter that have not melted over the fish, giving it a green coating. Give a quick baste with the winey juices and return to the oven for 5 minutes, or until the fish is just cooked through. To serve, slice the fish into four and spoon some juices over each serving. Oven-roasted potato wedges go well with this – simply scrub and cut the potatoes into wedges, season, roll in olive oil and place in the hot oven about 30 minutes before the fish. For veg, a stir-fry is great: green beans, button mushrooms, julienned baby marrows and carrots, chopped leeks – all good. **This fish dish will serve 4, and is easily doubled.**

POACHED FISH with anchovy mayo and crunchy sage

For this recipe you need just a side of fish. Kabeljou (kob) weighing 600–700 g is first choice.

COURT BOUILLON

1.25 litres (5 cups) water

125 ml (½ cup) off-dry white wine

1 large carrot cut into 4 pieces

1 onion, chunkily chopped

2 bay leaves

a few black peppercorns

5 ml (1 tsp) sea salt

a few sprigs of fresh parsley

ANCHOVY MAYONNAISE

1 x 40 g can fillets of anchovied sardines,
  briefly soaked in milk and snipped

125 ml (½ cup) thick mayonnaise

45 ml (3 Tbsp) thick Bulgarian yoghurt

a pinch of sugar

60 ml (4 Tbsp) chopped fresh flat-leaf parsley

2 ml (½ tsp) finely grated lemon rind

GARNISH

Heat a little oil in a frying pan and shallow-fry fresh sage leaves until they change colour and become crisp. Drain on paper towel and scatter over.

Bring all the bouillon ingredients to the boil, then cover and simmer for 30 minutes – you can do this in advance and leave to cool and draw flavour.

Place the fish, skin side down, in a wide pan so that it lies flat. Strain the bouillon over the fish (it should be almost covered) and poach very gently until just cooked and opaque – white, no longer pink (add a dash of verjuice to the liquid if you have some). When done, remove from heat and leave to cool in the bouillon. Use a spatula to transfer the fish to a large serving platter.

For the anchovy mayo, mix together the anchovies, mayonnaise, yoghurt and sugar. Whisk to 'melt' a little – don't whizz in a blender – and leave the dressing slightly speckled. Drizzle over the fish, then sprinkle with the parsley and lemon rind. Scatter the sage leaves over. **Serves 4.**

POACHED FISH with lemon and tarragon

This is stove-top fish without any frying. The subtle, delicately flavoured sauce in no way spoils the purity of fresh, white fish fillets and it's easy enough to serve for a supper treat when everyone is tired of fish and chips. Furthermore, both the stock and the butter can be put together in advance, leaving only the fish requiring last-minute attention. You can serve it on mash – or leave off the starch and present simply with a mixed salad or stir-fried veg.

5 ml (1 tsp) very finely grated lemon rind
5 ml (1 tsp) dried tarragon
500 ml (2 cups) water
125 ml (½ cup) white wine
5 ml (1 tsp) sea salt
6 slices (about 1 kg) white fish fillets, skinned
20 ml (4 tsp) Dijon mustard
30 ml (2 Tbsp) flour
30 ml (2 Tbsp) soft butter
60 ml (¼ cup) reduced-fat cream

Bring the lemon rind, tarragon, water, wine and salt to a slow boil in a very large, wide-based frying pan, then reduce the heat, cover and simmer for 10 minutes. Gently slide in the fish fillets, cover the pan, and poach gently until just cooked and the flesh flakes easily. Use a slotted spoon to transfer to a serving dish. Mash the mustard, flour and butter to a paste and add to the pan in single pats, while stirring. When thickened and smooth, swirl in the cream, then drizzle the sauce over the waiting fish.

Serves 6.

UNBELIEVABLY EASY FISH with salsa

This is quite the most fuss-free and unpretentious dish – the sort of recipe you like to turn to because it's so reliable and comfortable, like an old slipper. All you need is fresh hake and four ingredients to roll it in. Then, to jolly up the colour and flavour, quickly stir up a salsa – avos and Peppadews – and that's it.

30 ml (2 Tbsp) oil
20 ml (4 tsp) soy sauce
15 ml (1 Tbsp) white wine
5 ml (1 tsp) finely grated lemon rind
4 fresh, skinless hake fillets of equal thickness
(about 550 g)
pre-roasted sesame seeds for topping

SALSA
**Peppadews (mild, whole, sweet piquanté peppers
from a jar)**
1 large avocado, peeled and diced
a dash of fresh lemon juice
3–4 spring onions, chopped
a pinch of sea salt and milled black pepper
5 ml (1 tsp) olive oil

Using a fork, mix the oil, soy sauce, wine and lemon rind on a large plate. Turn the fish fillets in the mixture several times to coat them well, then place in a baking dish lined with baking paper and pour over any remaining soy mixture. Sprinkle with sesame seeds and bake at 200 °C for about 20 minutes, until just cooked through. If the juices have run, spoon them over the top of each fillet when serving, and pass a salt grinder – the soy sauce may season the fish sufficiently, but then again it may not, depending on the brand.

To make the salsa, snip enough Peppadews (rinsed and drained) to give you 45–60 ml (3–4 Tbsp). Gently mix with the remaining ingredients, pile into a small bowl and serve with the fish, or spoon a little of the salsa over the top for a colourful presentation.
Serves 4.

BAKED FISH FILLETS on a bed of vegetables

This is a splendid way of transforming hake into something quite special without any fuss, frying or fancy ingredients. It's a good and useful recipe, which can be used with other kinds of fish as well, except for oily fish like snoek. Although hake seems to pop up mainly in fish pies or under a coat of batter, it's first choice here because its delicate flavour responds to this kind of treatment and, being non-oily, it can take the topping of cheese and juicy sauce.

2 large onions, sliced across into thin rings
500 g ripe tomatoes, skinned and sliced into rings
sea salt, milled black pepper and a pinch of sugar
5 ml (1 tsp) dried dill, or dried tarragon, or mixed herbs
30 ml (2 Tbsp) olive oil
60 ml (¼ cup) white wine
4 fresh hake fillets (about 180 g each) or 1 large piece weighing about 720 g
a little fresh lemon juice and sea salt
mozzarella cheese, grated
paprika
extra 60 ml (¼ cup) white wine

Brush a large baking dish with oil and arrange the onion slices in a single layer to cover the base. Top with the sliced tomatoes and sprinkle with the seasonings and dried herb of choice. Drizzle with the oil and wine, then bake, uncovered, at 180 °C for 15 minutes. Place the fish on top of the semi-soft vegetables, sprinkle lightly with lemon juice and salt, then top with cheese and a flurry of paprika. Pour the extra wine round – not on – the fish and bake, uncovered, at the same temperature, for about 20 minutes more, or until the fish is just cooked, the cheese melted, and the vegetables soft and juicy. To serve, spoon the veg over each fillet, or alongside, and serve with baby potatoes tossed in garlic butter, and a green vegetable – broccoli is good because of the bright colour. **Serves 4.**

simply super **FISH DISH**

At heart this is a basic oldie from every Granny's cookbook: hake, mushroom sauce and cheese, but an updated spin results in something really special. In this recipe, chunky portabellini mushrooms add amazing texture to the creamy sauce, which is poured over a whole side of firm-textured yellowtail. The topping of cheddar remains, and the quick browning under the grill. If preferred, use another type of mushroom, or fish, but this combination is really good.

1 side of yellowtail, skinned and filleted, 600–700 g (prepared weight)
sea salt and fresh lemon juice
uncoloured, grated Cheddar cheese for topping

SAUCE
15 ml (1 Tbsp) oil and a nut of butter
1 bunch spring onions or 2 bunching onions, chopped
250 g portabellini mushrooms, wiped and quartered
a pinch of dried dill
30 ml (2 Tbsp) flour
375 ml (1½ cups) milk (preferably low-fat, it's a rich dish)
10 ml (2 tsp) Dijon mustard
10 ml (2 tsp) tomato paste
a pinch each of sea salt and sugar

Place the fish, skinned side up, in a lightly oiled baking dish in which it will lie flat. Season lightly and sprinkle with lemon juice, then bake at 180 °C until just cooked through; test with a fork – yellowtail, especially, dries out if overcooked.

While the fish is in the oven, make the sauce. Heat the oil and butter in a heavy saucepan, add the onions, mushrooms and dill, and cook, tossing gently over low heat, for several minutes, then sprinkle in the flour. When absorbed, slowly stir in the milk, then the mustard and tomato paste. Allow to bubble away over low heat for a few minutes until you have a medium-thick, faintly pink sauce. Season and pour the sauce over the cooked fish. Sprinkle modestly with cheese and slide under a preheated grill until golden brown. This happens quickly, so don't go away. Serve in neat slices with brown rice and a green veg, or a salad. **Serves 4.**

saucy, crumb-topped **BAKED FISH FILLETS**

Fresh fish fillets, covered with a nutty/crumby/herby mixture and baked on a mushroom-tomato sauce. Cape salmon and kabeljou (kob) are good choices. The fillets must be skinned, so that all the flavours can penetrate.

4 large, skinned fish fillets, about 700 g
sea salt and milled black pepper
slivers of butter

SAUCE
30 ml (2 Tbsp) oil
2 leeks, thinly sliced
250 g mushrooms, white or brown, wiped and chunked
400 g ripe and juicy tomatoes, skinned and chopped
sea salt, milled black pepper and a pinch of sugar

TOPPING
3 thin slices crustless, rather stale bread
1 slim slice onion
grated rind of ½ large lemon
24 unblanched almonds
a small handful of fresh parsley tufts
3 ml (a rounded ½ tsp) dried dill (or about 15 ml (1 Tbsp) chopped fresh dill)
15 ml (1 Tbsp) oil

To make the sauce, heat the oil and soften the leeks, then add the remaining ingredients. Cover and simmer for 15 minutes, stirring now and then to mash up the tomatoes; the result should be a juicy sauce, not thick. Pour into a baking dish to cover the base quite thickly.

For the topping, put the bread, onion, lemon rind, almonds and herbs into the bowl of a processor fitted with the metal blade. Process until finely crumbed, then add the oil and pulse until moistened. Place the fish on the tomato sauce and season, then spread the crumb mixture over the top of each fillet, patting down lightly. Arrange a few slivers of butter on top and bake at 180 °C for 25–30 minutes until the fish is cooked through. Serve with the sauce and a green veg or salad and, if that's not enough, you could boil a few potatoes, slice them into wedges, brush with a little oil and bake at the same time as the fish. **Serves 4.**

CHICKEN

spicy indian-style
BUTTER CHICKEN

This dish really does taste as good as it looks: tender nuggets of chicken in a smooth red sauce, fresh green coriander and saffron-tinted basmati rice. Skinless thigh fillets are perfect here – unlike breast fillets, they won't dry out despite the long, slow simmer. The dish may be made a day ahead and chilled overnight.

**2 x 410 g cans Indian Diced Tomatoes
(with curry leaves and spices)
45 ml (3 Tbsp) oil
1.2 kg skinless chicken thigh fillets
60 g butter
10 ml (2 tsp) each ground cumin, curry powder
and paprika
5 ml (1 tsp) ground cinnamon
about 20 ml (4 tsp) finely chopped, peeled root ginger
a pinch of crushed dried chillies (optional)
about 10 ml (2 tsp) sea salt
15 ml (1 Tbsp) sugar
a little fresh lemon juice, if necessary
90 ml (6 Tbsp) thick plain yoghurt
10 ml (2 tsp) garam masala and a handful of fresh
coriander or curry leaves to garnish**

Empty the tomatoes into a blender and whizz until smooth, then set aside. Heat the oil in a deep, wide saucepan. Add the chicken, toss until just sealed and pale beige on both sides, then remove and set aside. Immediately reduce the heat to very low, add the butter and, when melted, sprinkle in the ground spices and ginger. Sizzle briefly until aromatic, then return the chicken to the saucepan and mix in the blended tomatoes, as well as the chillies, salt and sugar. At this stage the mixture will seem too thick, but don't add any liquid, the sauce will soon thin out sufficiently. Cover and simmer very gently, stirring now and then, for 50–60 minutes, or until the chicken is very tender and the sauce medium-thick and richly coloured. If the flavour needs a little lift, add a dash of lemon juice, then swirl in the yoghurt, sprinkle with the garnishes, and heat through without boiling. Ladle the chicken and sauce alongside servings of saffron basmati rice, and accompany with a bright green vegetable or salad. **Serves 6–8.**

CHICKEN AND MANGO salad

An eye-catching combination of bright ingredients goes into this salad of chicken poached in apple juice,
mixed into a creamy curry sauce together with fresh mangoes, and finished off with nuts and coriander.
It can be made in advance and refrigerated overnight. Serve with a rice or couscous salad and
a mild fruit chutney – atchars would be too strong for the delicate flavour.

500–600 g skinless free-range chicken breast fillets
250 ml (1 cup) apple juice
2 whole cloves
a little sea salt
1 stick cinnamon
2 medium, firm, ripe fibreless mangoes, peeled and diced
chopped walnuts/pecans and fresh coriander to garnish

DRESSING
30 ml (2 Tbsp) oil
1 medium onion, finely chopped
15 ml (1 Tbsp) curry powder
5 ml (1 tsp) turmeric
125 ml (½ cup) reserved chicken stock
125 ml (½ cup) mayonnaise
125 ml (½ cup) sour cream or thick Bulgarian yoghurt

Poach the chicken gently in apple juice with the cloves, salt and cinnamon for about 10 minutes, or until just cooked. Cool in the stock, then slice the chicken into thin strips across the grain. Strain the stock and reserve.

To make the dressing, heat the oil in a small saucepan. Add the onion and let it soften without browning. Add the spices and sizzle for a minute, then add the reserved stock and simmer, uncovered, until the mixture thickens – this happens quite quickly. Press through a sieve, discard the onion, and stir the smooth sauce into the mayonnaise mixed with the sour cream or yoghurt. Fold in the chicken, then the mango, spoon into a glass container, cover and refrigerate. Before serving, check the seasoning and, if too sweet, sharpen with a little fresh lemon juice. Spoon onto a beautiful platter, and garnish with the nuts and a generous sprinkling of coriander leaves. **Serves 6–8.**

BUCKINGHAM CHICKEN with litchis and almonds

This is a new take on Coronation Chicken. It's quicker, easier and lighter, without compromising on the splendid flavour of cold chicken in a creamy curry sauce.

4 large free-range chicken breasts (about 900 g),
with bone and skin
500 ml (2 cups) water
a few slices of onion
a few sprigs of fresh parsley
5 ml (1 tsp) turmeric
2–3 bay leaves
a sprinkling of sea salt
a large bunch of spring onions, chopped
1 x 410 g can pitted litchis, drained, slivered, patted dry
toasted almond flakes to garnish

DRESSING
250 ml (1 cup) thick plain low-fat or fat-free yoghurt
250 ml (1 cup) choice, thick mayonnaise
45–60 ml (3–4 Tbsp) curry paste (not powder)
about 5 ml (1 tsp) honey

Poach the chicken in the water with the onion, parsley, turmeric, bay leaves and salt. Cook gently, turning once, and, when done, leave to cool in the stock. Pull off the flesh with your fingers, shredding it and discarding the skin, bone and gristle. Place in a bowl, mix in the spring onions and litchis, then drizzle over about 125 ml (½ cup) strained stock. The chicken flesh will slowly absorb the stock; when it starts to run to the base of the bowl, add no more.

To make the dressing, mix the yoghurt, mayonnaise and curry paste (start with 45 ml) with the honey (even a touch of honey rounds out the flavour, particularly if you have used fat-free yoghurt). Taste and add more curry paste if wanted, then pour two-thirds of the dressing over the chicken, tossing gently until combined. Cover and refrigerate for a few hours, or overnight; refrigerate the extra dressing as well. To serve, spoon the chicken onto a large platter, pour the extra dressing over the top (or serve separately), and finish off with almonds. Serve with chutney, a rice or couscous salad, and something green. **Serves 6.**

quick CHICKEN OREGANO

Marinate it, bake it, and out comes chicken with loads of flavour. This incredibly simple dish requires minimal effort and only a few ingredients, yet it's always relished and a treasure for the busy cook. You could use chicken pieces, as in a braai pack, but thighs are the best for succulence, and they'll all cook through at the same time. Serve hot with a platter of roasted vegetables and yoghurt, or at room temperature with a Greek salad for a patio picnic.

8 chicken thighs (about 1 kg), trimmed of excess fat
60 ml (¼ cup) olive oil
3–4 cloves garlic, crushed
15 ml (1 Tbsp) dried oregano
60 ml (¼ cup) dry white wine
1 ml (¼ tsp) ground cinnamon
10 ml (2 tsp) runny honey
sea salt and milled black pepper

Make two slashes on the skin side of each thigh. Mix together the remaining ingredients, except the salt and pepper, in a shallow baking dish; add the chicken, skin side down, and refrigerate for 2–3 hours, turning once. Place the thighs on the oiled rack of a grill pan, skin side up, pour the marinade over, and then season each piece. Add a little hot water to the grill pan to prevent scorching and to keep the chicken moist, then bake at 180 °C for 50–60 minutes, or until well browned and cooked through, adding extra hot water to the pan whenever necessary. It is important to keep the liquid topped up in order to provide succulent juices to pour over the cooked thighs. Arrange on a warmed serving platter, pour pan juices over, and serve. **Serves 4–6.**

CITRUS CHICKEN BAKE with minted pesto pasta

Deliciously different, yet perfectly straightforward, this dish is an exciting way of treating basic ingredients.

900 g–1 kg free-range chicken pieces, excess fat removed

30 ml (2 Tbsp) olive oil

3–4 cloves garlic, chopped

2 pickling onions, chopped

about 15 ml (1 Tbsp) chopped rosemary leaves

150 ml (⅗ cup) fresh orange juice

coarsely grated rind of ½ orange

30 ml (2 Tbsp) honey

45 ml (3 Tbsp) white vermouth

15 ml (1 Tbsp) wholegrain mustard

coarsely grated rind of 1 medium lemon

5 ml (1 tsp) sea salt

200 g pasta shells

Discard the wing tips. Place the chicken, flesh side down, to fit closely in a dish suitable for marinating and baking. Whizz the remaining ingredients, except the pasta, in a blender, and pour over the chicken. Leave for 30 minutes. Cover with a lid, or greaseproof paper and then foil, and bake at 180 °C for 45 minutes. Turn and bake, uncovered, for a further 35–40 minutes until the chicken is tender and brown. Skim off the fat. Cook the pasta, then drain it in a colander set over a bowl. Return the pasta to the saucepan with a spoon of the cooking water, and stir in enough pesto to gloss and flavour. Serve immediately. Drizzle the sauce from the baking dish over the chicken and spoon the pasta alongside.

Serves 4.

PESTO

250 ml (1 cup) fresh mint leaves, rinsed and dried

250 ml (1 cup) fresh parsley tufts, firmly packed

20 g walnuts, roughly chopped

30 ml (2 Tbsp) grated Parmesan or pecorino cheese

1 clove garlic, chopped

90 ml (6 Tbsp) olive oil

Place all the ingredients, except the oil, in the bowl of a processor fitted with the metal blade. Pulse until finely chopped, then drizzle in the oil, scraping down the sides – the pesto should be thick and chunky.

CHICKEN CURRY with brown mushrooms and tomato

The favourite. Everyone seems to love this curry. There's nothing exceptional in the ingredients,
yet somehow they marry so happily that seconds are requested, all round, every time.

15 ml (1 Tbsp) each oil and butter

8 large (1 kg) free-range chicken thighs, trimmed

sea salt and milled black pepper

1 large onion, finely chopped

4 cloves garlic, crushed

30 ml (2 Tbsp) curry powder

10 ml (2 tsp) ground cumin

5 ml (1 tsp) turmeric

15 ml (1 Tbsp) peeled, chopped fresh root ginger

250 g brown mushrooms, wiped and sliced

1 x 410 g can whole tomatoes, chopped, plus juice

2 fat sticks cinnamon

3 bay leaves

about 5 ml (1 tsp) sugar

45 ml (3 Tbsp) chutney

125 ml (½ cup) hot, seasoned chicken stock

a small handful of fresh coriander leaves

Heat the oil and butter in a large pan and brown the
chicken on both sides – fry skin side first to release
the fat. Transfer to a large baking dish (28 x 22 cm is
just right) and remove the skins (the chicken will
absorb the flavours better and it avoids a greasy
sauce). Turn skinned sides down and season lightly.
The thighs should fit fairly closely, but allow space
for the chunky sauce. Add the onion, garlic, ground
spices and ginger to the pan drippings and sauté
briefly over low heat – if necessary, add a dash of
water. Add the mushrooms, toss until mixed with the
spices, then add the remaining ingredients, except
the coriander. Bring to the boil, stirring, then pour
over the chicken. Tuck in the cinnamon and bay
leaves, cover securely (greaseproof paper and then
foil) and bake at 160 °C for 1¼ hours. Turn the chicken
and bake, uncovered, for a further 15 minutes, or
until tender and the sauce is reduced. Use a slotted
spoon to transfer the thighs to a heated serving dish,
remove the bay leaves and cinnamon, swirl in the
coriander, pour the sauce over the chicken and serve
with a fragrant rice and thick yoghurt. **Serves 4–6.**

CHICKEN AND AUBERGINE casserole with herbs

If you love Greek-style ingredients, this one is for you. You need only a smattering of pine nuts, but even then they are expensive, and feta cheese can be substituted very successfully.

olive oil
1 kg chicken thighs, trimmed of excess fat
1 large onion, finely chopped
400 g aubergines (brinjals), washed, cubed, dégorged
and patted dry
4 cloves garlic, chopped
400 g tomatoes, skinned and chopped
45 ml (3 Tbsp) flour
375 ml (1½ cups) hot chicken stock
15–30 ml (1–2 Tbsp) honey
2 sprigs of fresh rosemary
30 ml (2 Tbsp) brandy
a little sea salt
125 ml (½ cup) chopped fresh mixed herbs*
a scattering of lightly toasted pine nuts,
or 100 g feta cheese, crumbled

Brush a frying pan with olive oil. Add the chicken, skin side down, and brown well, then turn and lightly brown the other side. Remove to a baking dish, large and deep enough to take the chunky sauce, arranging the chicken skin side down. Add the onion, aubergines, garlic and tomatoes to the pan, adding a splash of water if the drippings have disappeared. Stir over low heat until just softening, then sprinkle in the flour and, when absorbed, stir in the stock, honey, rosemary, brandy and salt. Pour over the chicken – it will disappear completely under the sauce – then cover with a lid, or a sheet of greaseproof paper and then foil. Bake at 180 °C for 15 minutes, then reduce the heat to 160 °C and bake for a further 45 minutes. Turn the thighs right side up and bake, uncovered, for 30 minutes until tender and the sauce is bright, thick and bubbly. Sprinkle with the herbs and nuts or feta, and return to the oven, still uncovered, for 10 minutes. **Serves 6.**

* Chopped parsley, mint and oregano in the ratio of half parsley and quarter each mint and oregano.

CHICKEN WITH RED WINE,
figs and walnuts

The gorgeous depth of colour and explosion of spicy flavours make this chicken dish quite different from any other. It really is most unusual, and deeply delicious served with a Greek salad without the feta, and a grain, or orzo (small barley-shaped pasta).

8 large (about 1.2 kg) chicken thighs
30 ml (2 Tbsp) flour
7 ml (1½ tsp) dried oregano
5 ml (1 tsp) sea salt
30 ml (2 Tbsp) olive oil
1 large onion, finely chopped
5 ml (1 tsp) each ground cinnamon and coriander
1 ml (¼ tsp) ground allspice (pimento)
300 ml (1⅕ cups) seasoned chicken stock
125 ml (½ cup) red wine (a mature claret is good)
2 bay leaves
6–8 (about 130 g) ready-to-eat, soft dried figs, quartered
coarsely grated rind of 1 lemon (use a zester if possible)
coarsely chopped walnuts and parsley for topping

Remove the skin from the thighs. Once skinned, weigh – you should have 1 kg. Mix the flour, oregano and salt. Make two or three slashes on the skinned side of each thigh, and rub with the flour mixture (do the reverse side as well, although it's too bony to slash). Heat the oil in a large frying pan and brown the thighs lightly on both sides – do this in batches and then arrange in a baking dish, skinned side down, and quite closely together, but with space for the generous sauce. Add the onion to the frying pan and, if necessary, a dash more oil. Add the spices. Toss over a low heat and, when fabulously aromatic, add the stock, wine and bay leaves. Bring to the boil, pour over the chicken, cover securely with a sheet of greaseproof paper, and then a lid or foil. Bake at 160 °C for 1 hour. Turn the pieces, mix in the figs and lemon rind, and bake, uncovered, for a further 30 minutes; the sauce should be dark and fairly thick, the chicken tender and succulent. Check the seasoning – it may need salt and perhaps a squeeze of fresh lemon juice. Sprinkle with the topping, return to the oven for just 5 minutes, then serve.
Serves 6–8.

CHICKEN THIGHS
baked on a bed of vegetables

There's a lovely harmony of tastes and textures in this chicken dish, which is initially baked covered, to seal in all the flavours and juices, and then uncovered in order to brown the chicken. The completed dish is a picture to make your mouth water – and although the assembly time is quite lengthy, once it's done you can relax.

2 medium onions, peeled and quartered
300 g baby marrows, pared and sliced into strips
1 large red pepper, seeded, ribs removed, and sliced
2 x 200 g aubergines (brinjals), scrubbed and cubed*
400 g tomatoes (skin on), quartered
200 g brown mushrooms, wiped and thickly sliced
12 cloves garlic, unpeeled
60 ml (¼ cup) olive oil
sea salt, milled black pepper and a large pinch of sugar
3–4 sprigs of fresh rosemary
6 large (800 g) free-range chicken thighs, trimmed of excess fat
paprika and dried oregano

Use a very large, deep baking dish, round about 36 x 26 x 5 cm. Add all the vegetables, toss with 45 ml (3 Tbsp) of the oil (use your hands), and when glistening, season and tuck in the rosemary. Place the chicken thighs, skin side up, on the vegetables, not too close to each other, and push them down very gently – they must not be smothered. Salt them lightly and sprinkle with paprika and oregano. Cover securely, first with a sheet of greaseproof paper and then foil, and bake at 160 °C for 1 hour. Uncover and bake for 45 minutes, or until the chicken is gloriously brown and tender, in a succulent sauce. Remove the rosemary, and serve the chicken and veg on rice or couscous to soak up the juices. Don't forget to locate the garlic cloves: place two on each plate so that diners can squeeze the mellow flesh into the vegetables. **Serves 6.**

* If using one large aubergine it should be dégorged: scrub, cube, sprinkle with salt, place in a colander with a weight on top, leave for about 40 minutes while the bitter juices run out, then rinse well and dry thoroughly (a salad spinner does the job perfectly).

orange **COQ AU VIN**

A simplified version of the classic dish, with a new flip to the flavour.

15 ml (1 Tbsp) oil and a dab of butter

1 kg free-range chicken portions, preferably trimmed thighs and drumsticks

sea salt and milled black pepper

3–4 rashers lean shoulder bacon, diced

12 pickling onions, peeled

2–3 cloves garlic, crushed

30 ml (2 Tbsp) flour

2 ml (½ tsp) dried thyme

175 ml (⅔ cup) red wine

125 ml (½ cup) fresh orange juice

5 ml (1 tsp) finely grated orange rind

30 ml (2 Tbsp) brandy

15 ml (1 Tbsp) tomato paste

60 ml (¼ cup) chicken stock

5 ml (1 tsp) honey

2 bay leaves

200 g button mushrooms, halved

chopped parsley to garnish

Heat the oil and butter and brown the chicken on both sides. Remove to a baking dish – not too large, or the sauce will boil away, but large enough to take the rather bulky ingredients. Season. Over low heat, toss the bacon, onions and garlic in the pan drippings and, when the onions are lightly browned, sprinkle in the flour and thyme (crush the thyme between your fingers). When absorbed, add the remaining ingredients, except the mushrooms and garnish. Stir until boiling, then pour the sauce over the chicken, tucking in the onions. Cover securely with a lid or with a sheet of greaseproof paper and then one of foil, and bake at 160 °C for 1¼ hours. Stir in the mushrooms and bake, uncovered, for 15 minutes. Use a paper towel to blot up any little greasy blobs, remove the bay leaves and sprinkle with parsley. **Serves 4–5.**

finger-licking **CHICKEN WINGS**

Chicken wings are often neglected – I suppose because there's not much meat on them – but they're succulent and jolly useful. In the following recipe they're marinated in a barbecue-type sauce, which adds great colour and flavour. Once cooked, they can be served as an economical main course with the juices spooned over, accompanied by baked potatoes and sour cream; alternatively, drain off the juices and serve with drinks; or grill over the coals and pass them round for nibbling to appease appetites.

1 kg free-range chicken wings
30 ml (2 Tbsp) oil
45 ml (3 Tbsp) sweet sherry
45 ml (3 Tbsp) tomato sauce
30 ml (2 Tbsp) fresh lemon juice
5 ml (1 tsp) Worcestershire sauce
15 ml (1 Tbsp) soy sauce
10 ml (2 tsp) pale, runny honey
10 ml (2 tsp) curry powder
10 ml (2 tsp) chilli sauce (or more for extra bite)
sea salt and milled black pepper

Remove the wing tips if your butcher has not already done so, then pull the wings apart and cut through at the joint, making two pieces. Be careful not to cut through the bone, leaving a jagged edge, but at the precise point where the joint separates. Arrange in a single layer in a large glass or porcelain baking dish – 30 x 24 cm is ideal. Mix the remaining ingredients, except the salt and pepper, pour over the wings and leave to stand for 30 minutes at room temperature, or refrigerate for up to 6 hours, turning several times. Unless using a fridge-to-oven baking dish, return to room temperature before baking. Season very lightly, and bake, uncovered, at 180 °C for 25 minutes. Turn the pieces over and add a little water to the baking dish if necessary, to prevent scorching. Reduce the heat to 160 °C and bake for a further 25 minutes, or until tender, browned and juicy. **Makes about 32 pieces, serving 5–6 as a main.**

favourite **QUICK CHICKEN**

This lemony, herby, spicy chicken (memories of the Med) is just the best when it comes to kitchen blues.
When dinner is required and you are absolutely not in the mood for pots and wooden spoons,
your energy is flagging and you'd rather be in the garden, let this recipe save you.

800 g free-range chicken thighs, trimmed of excess fat
a little sea salt

MARINADE
60 ml (¼ cup) fresh lemon juice
30 ml (2 Tbsp) olive oil
30 ml (2 Tbsp) brandy
15 ml (1 Tbsp) runny honey
2 cloves garlic, crushed
7 ml (1½ tsp) ground cumin
7 ml (1½ tsp) dried oregano
2 ml (½ tsp) ground cinnamon

Arrange the chicken in a baking dish to fit closely.
Mix all the ingredients for the marinade, pour over
the chicken and refrigerate for 1–4 hours, turning a
few times. Unless using a fridge-to-oven baking dish,
return to room temperature before baking. Arrange
the thighs, skin side up, salt lightly, and bake,
uncovered, at 160 °C for 45 minutes. Baste with the
juices in the dish, then continue baking for a further
25 minutes or until the chicken is browned and
tender. Transfer to a warmed platter and pour the
juices over. **Serves 4.**

baked **SPICY CHICKEN**

A perennial favourite, abundantly perfumed and flavoured.

45 ml (3 Tbsp) flour
7 ml (1½ tsp) salt
5 ml (1 tsp) garam masala
8 large (not less than 1 kg) free-range, skinless
chicken thighs*
30 ml (2 Tbsp) oil
2 medium onions, chopped
2–3 cloves garlic, crushed
10 ml (2 tsp) chopped, peeled fresh root ginger
15 ml (1 Tbsp) curry powder
5 ml (1 tsp) each ground cumin and turmeric
3 whole star anise
2 sticks cinnamon
300 ml (1⅕ cups) chicken stock
125 ml (½ cup) tomato purée
2 bay leaves
60 ml (4 Tbsp) seedless raisins
30 ml (2 Tbsp) chutney
fresh coriander leaves to garnish

* Skinless thighs absorb flavours readily and ensure a non-fatty sauce.

Mix the flour, salt and masala, rub it into the chicken, arrange in a lightly oiled baking dish to fit quite snugly and sprinkle over any remaining flour mixture. Heat the oil, add the onions, garlic and ginger and fry lightly, then add all the spices and stir over low heat until the aroma escapes – if necessary, add a dash of water to prevent scorching. Add the remaining ingredients, except the garnish, stir while heating through, then pour the sauce over the chicken. Check that the spices lie in the sauce and not on top of the thighs, then cover securely with a lid or a sheet of greaseproof paper and then one of foil, and bake at 160 °C for 45 minutes. Turn the chicken, cover again, and bake for a further 30 minutes, or until tender. Remove the whole spices and bay leaves, transfer to a heated serving dish and sprinkle with coriander leaves. **Serves 4–6.**

tarragon and lemon cream CHICKEN BREASTS

Subtly flavoured and richly sauced, this is stove-top chicken at its elegant best. Surprisingly few ingredients are required, and the chief players – lemon grass, honey and crème fraîche – combine quite brilliantly.

4 (about 400 g) skinless chicken breast fillets

15 ml (1 Tbsp) oil and a small pat of butter

375 ml (1½ cups) chicken stock (home-made is best)

4–6 spring onions, chopped

5 ml (1 tsp) dried tarragon

5 ml (1 tsp) very finely grated lemon rind

2 stalks lemon grass (whole white lower stems,
**   outer layer peeled)**

15 ml (1 Tbsp) runny honey

2 ml (½ tsp) sea salt

75–90 ml (5–6 Tbsp) crème fraîche*

Make a few shallow slashes on the skinned side of the chicken, then flatten the breasts slightly by thumping gently with a rolling pin – be careful not to tear them. Heat the oil and butter in a large frying pan and seal the chicken on both sides; do this quickly – they must not brown at all. Remove from the pan and set aside. Lower the heat and add the stock, spring onions, tarragon (crush with your fingers as you sprinkle it in), lemon rind, lemon grass, honey and salt to the pan. Stir, then simmer, half covered, for 12–15 minutes until slightly thickened and reduced. Discard the lemon grass and stir in 75 ml (5 Tbsp) of the crème fraîche and, when smoothly combined, return the chicken to the pan. Cover and simmer gently until the chicken is cooked through – 6 minutes. The sauce should be medium-thick and fairly generous, so if it reduced too much at the start, you might want to add more crème fraîche, or a little extra stock – at this stage you have to play it by ear, at the same time being careful not to mask the delicate flavour of the sauce. When you're happy, serve. Rice timbales (rice cooked in stock with bright things added, like parsley and red pepper, then moulded and unmoulded) are not much trouble to make, and suit the dish well. **Serves 4.**

* If unobtainable, substitute cultured sour cream.

quick **MUSHROOM CHICKEN**

An old-timer, slipped in because it's so eternally useful: breast fillets quickly simmered in a delicately flavoured sauce with a hint of tarragon and sherry, and a little cream to round it off. The whole operation takes about 20 minutes and this makes the dish a real pleasure to prepare at the end of a busy day. Instead of reducing the sauce by rapid boiling, it is thickened with cornflour – not a gourmet practice, but convenient – and the breasts turn out plump and succulent. So it's easy, and good.

30 ml (2 Tbsp) oil

5 ml (1 tsp) butter

6 (about 600 g) skinless chicken breast fillets

6 slim spring onions, chopped

7 ml (1½ tsp) dried tarragon

60 ml (¼ cup) sweet sherry (OB's is perfect)

250 ml (1 cup) hot chicken stock

10 ml (2 tsp) tomato paste

250 g button mushrooms, wiped and sliced

a little sea salt

10 ml (2 tsp) cornflour

60 ml (¼ cup) cream (reduced-fat cream works well)

You'll need a really large frying pan so that nothing need be done in relays. Heat the oil and butter, make three diagonal slashes on the skinned sides of the breasts, and quickly seal on both sides; don't brown them – they should just turn white on the outsides and remain very pink underneath. Remove from the pan, reduce the heat, add the spring onions, tarragon and sherry, stir until almost evaporated, then add the stock, tomato paste, mushrooms and salt. Stir until just bubbling, then return the chicken, cover, and simmer over very low heat for about 10 minutes, or until just cooked through, turning once. Slake the cornflour with the cream, add to the pan and simmer for a minute or two to make a medium-thick sauce, stirring gently to combine. Check the seasoning.

Serves 6.

CHICKEN CASSEROLE with mushrooms and red wine

An unpretentious but deliciously satisfying chicken dish, with a full-bodied flavour.
The ingredients are quite basic, and the preparation not too quick, but straightforward.

12 pickling onions, peeled

1 kg free-range chicken thighs, trimmed of excess fat

2 ml (½ tsp) each salt and paprika

1 small onion, chopped

1 red pepper, seeded, ribs removed, and diced

250 g brown mushrooms, wiped and sliced

2 ml (½ tsp) dried thyme

30 ml (2 Tbsp) flour

250 ml (1 cup) chicken stock

100 ml (⅖ cup) robust red wine

15 ml (1 Tbsp) tomato paste

2 ml (½ tsp) sea salt and a little sugar

5 ml (1 tsp) Worcestershire sauce

Cut a cross through the root end of each pickling onion, arrange in a single layer in a large frying pan, half-cover with cold, lightly salted water, add a pinch of sugar and bring to the boil. Reduce the heat and simmer for about 8 minutes, then drain and set aside. (Don't boil rapidly, or overcook, as they must retain their shape.) Smear the base of a frying pan with a little oil and lightly brown the chicken on both sides – do the skin side first to release the fat. Arrange the thighs, skin side up, in a baking dish to fit, and sprinkle with salt and paprika. Cover with a lid, or a sheet of greaseproof paper and then one of foil, and bake at 160 °C for 30 minutes. Meanwhile, make the sauce. Add the chopped onion and red pepper to the pan drippings and sauté briefly. Add the mushrooms and thyme and a little extra oil if necessary, and stir-fry until softened. Sprinkle in the flour, tossing to mix, then add the remaining ingredients, stirring until the sauce thickens. Remove the chicken from the oven, uncover, and pour off the fat. Pour the sauce over and tuck in the parboiled pickling onions. Cover as before and bake for a further 45 minutes, or until the chicken is tender.
Serves 4–6.

CHOCOLATE-CHILLI chicken

The chilli bites only slightly, the chocolate is only subtly there, but the combination of ingredients adds up to an exciting medley of flavours that come as a happy surprise, because the dish looks like chicken in a richly coloured sauce ... yet it definitely is more than that. Really quick to prepare, and perfect with couscous – add a touch of turmeric and a small handful of currants when preparing.

375 ml (1½ cups) seasoned chicken stock

2 fresh red chillies, seeded and sliced*

2 medium ripe tomatoes, skinned, seeds flicked out, and chopped

a bunch of spring onions or a few baby leeks, chopped

2 ml (½ tsp) ground cinnamon

a little sea salt and a good pinch of sugar

30 ml (2 Tbsp) pre-toasted almond flakes, crushed**

60 ml (4 Tbsp) finely grated dark chocolate (about 25 g)

4 large (about 500 g) skinless chicken breast fillets

fresh coriander to garnish

* If you love the heat of chillies, use three, or don't de-seed.

** Use a rolling pin to crush – the almonds will stick a bit due to the oil, but simply scrape off the crumbs with a knife.

Place the stock, chillies, tomatoes, spring onions or leeks, cinnamon and seasonings in a blender goblet and pulse until well mixed, but not absolutely smooth. Pour into a large jug and stir in the almonds and chocolate, then pour into a medium-sized, heavy frying pan, with its base brushed with oil. Bring to the boil, then reduce the heat immediately. Make a few fairly deep slashes on the skinned side of each chicken breast, and slide into the pan, spoon some sauce over each, and then simmer gently, covered, until just cooked through, turning the chicken after 5 minutes. The breasts should be done in about 10 minutes – no longer pink in the middle, but soft and succulent. Using a slotted spoon, remove the chicken and reduce the sauce by increasing the heat and allowing it to boil rapidly, uncovered, for just a few minutes until slightly thickened and syrupy – this happens very quickly, so watch carefully else you might lose too much of it, which would be a great pity. Now either pour it over the waiting chicken, to coat each piece generously, or return the chicken, scatter with coriander, and serve from the pan, spooning a generous ladleful of sauce over each breast. **Serves 4.**

CHICKEN BREASTS stuffed with spinach and ricotta

There are four steps: mixing the stuffing, slipping it into the breasts, making the tomato sauce, then adding the chicken and simmering until cooked. Plenty of flavour and colour, and good with buttered noodles and a green salad.

100 g baby spinach leaves

100 g ricotta cheese

2 ml (½ tsp) freshly grated nutmeg

a large pinch of sea salt

6 (about 600 g) skinless chicken breast fillets

shavings of Parmesan or pecorino cheese for topping

TOMATO SAUCE

1 x 410 g can Italian-style sliced tomatoes

4–6 spring onions, chopped

1 large carrot, very finely diced

300 ml (1⅕ cups) chicken stock

30 ml (2 Tbsp) olive oil

2–3 cloves garlic, crushed

5 ml (1 tsp) tomato paste

a handful of chopped fresh parsley

5–10 ml (1–2 tsp) sugar

Pour boiling water over the spinach, leave to stand for 5 minutes, then drain well; press down hard with a spoon until absolutely dry – pat with a paper towel to make sure – then chop – you should have 60 ml (¼ cup) packed solid. Using a fork, mash the spinach with the ricotta and seasonings. Cut a deep vertical slit in the plump side of each chicken breast, being careful not to puncture the flaps. Ease open, and smooth a heaped tablespoon of the stuffing into each pocket. Close the flap and pinch securely.

Make the sauce by mixing all the ingredients in a very large pan, wide enough to take the breasts later on, without crowding. Bring to the boil, then reduce heat and simmer, covered, for 30 minutes, stirring occasionally, until fairly thick and the flavours have mellowed – salt is not usually necessary. Add the chicken, ladle some sauce over each breast, then cover and simmer for 10 minutes. Turn carefully, then continue to simmer until cooked through – about 20 minutes altogether. Serve the chicken on heated plates with the sauce spooned over, and topped with a sprinkling of cheese to round it all off. **Serves 6.**

SAUCY CHICKEN casserole

Colourful comfort food – everyday ingredients, lots of sauce, slightly tangy, slightly sweet and perfect with mash and veg.

a dash of oil
1–1.2 kg braai pack of free-range chicken, trimmed
sea salt and milled black pepper
1 large onion, finely chopped
2 medium carrots, finely diced
45 ml (3 Tbsp) flour
250 ml (1 cup) chicken stock
1 x 410 g can chopped, peeled tomatoes
15 ml (1 Tbsp) tomato paste
30 ml (2 Tbsp) wholegrain mustard
45 ml (3 Tbsp) Mrs Ball's chutney
10 ml (2 tsp) Worcestershire sauce
20 ml (4 tsp) caramel brown sugar
60 ml (4 Tbsp) seedless raisins
chopped fresh parsley for sprinkling

Heat just a slick of oil in a frying pan and brown the chicken lightly, skin side first to release any excess fat. Arrange the pieces, skin side down and fairly close together, in a large baking dish, deep enough to take the generous sauce. Season lightly. Add the onion and carrots to the pan drippings and toss over a low heat until just starting to colour and soften, then sprinkle in the flour. When absorbed, add the stock, tomatoes, tomato paste, mustard, chutney, Worcestershire sauce, sugar, raisins and a little salt. Stir to mix while bringing to the boil. Pour over the chicken, which should be almost completely covered by the sauce. Cover the dish with a lid, or with a sheet of greaseproof paper and then foil, and bake at 160 °C for 1¼ hours. Turn the chicken pieces, increase the oven temperature to 180 °C and bake, uncovered, for a further 15–20 minutes. If the sauce looks at all greasy, simply flick a paper kitchen towel over the top. Sprinkle with parsley and serve. **Serves 5–6.**

MEAT
venison, ostrich, beef, veal, lamb, pork

VENISON STEW
with allesverloren and prunes

In the old days, game was marinated for days before cooking it, to tone down the gamey, outright hairy flavour. But that was then. Now, with butchers selling farm-reared, young springbok, it's a different story – marinating is often skipped, and fillets and steaks served rare. Not so in this dish, in which the rules are bent, and steaks are given the old-fashioned treatment – a slow, well-done simmer. The result is fabulous: soft, tender chunks of meat in a richly flavoured gravy, glossed with jelly. This is stove-top cooking, which means you can check and stir whenever necessary, and it can all be done in advance – in fact it's even more delicious the next day. Serve with clapshot – a weird and wonderful name for a simple dish of mash from the chilly islands to the north of Scotland. There, it is usually served with sausages, but it goes very well with this venison stew, and makes a welcome change from the traditional yellow rice.

4 x 200 g boneless venison steaks from a young springbok leg

30 ml (2 Tbsp) red wine vinegar

150 g pitted prunes, halved

100 ml (⅖ cup) Allesverloren port

oil and butter for browning

2 large onions, finely chopped

4 rashers unsmoked back bacon, diced

2 medium carrots, diced

30 ml (2 Tbsp) flour

600 ml (2⅖ cups) hot, seasoned beef stock

extra 60 ml (¼ cup) Allesverloren port

15 ml (1 Tbsp) tomato paste

spices and seasoning: 3 whole cloves, 2 bay leaves, 2 sticks cinnamon, a large pinch of ground allspice, 2 x 5 cm strips lemon peel, and a little sea salt

15 ml (1 Tbsp) quince jelly

Using a sharp knife, pull off any thin membrane round the steaks. Pour the vinegar into a glass dish, add the steaks, turn over and over until coated, and leave for 1–2 hours. Place the prunes in a shallow dish and cover with the port. Wipe the steaks dry and slice each into three or four chunks. Heat the oil and butter in a large, wide saucepan and brown the meat well on both sides. Remove and set aside. Reduce the heat, add a little extra oil to the pan, then add the onions, bacon and carrots and, when soft and golden, sprinkle in the flour. When absorbed, stir in the stock, extra port, tomato paste and all the spices and seasoning. Return the meat to the saucepan, cover, and simmer over low heat for 1 hour, then stir in the prunes and port and simmer for another 30 minutes.

Finally, stir in the jelly to work its magic. Serve immediately or cool, turn into a suitable container, and refrigerate overnight. Add a little extra stock if necessary to thin out the gravy. **Serves 4–5.**

CLAPSHOT

300 g medium turnips, peeled and sliced (prepared weight)

500 g potatoes, peeled and cubed (prepared weight)

30 ml (2 Tbsp) butter

15 ml (1 Tbsp) oil

3 medium leeks, shredded

a pinch of freshly grated nutmeg

sea salt and white pepper to taste

warm milk

Cook the prepared turnips in a little boiling salted water for 15 minutes. Add the potatoes and boil together until both vegetables are soft, adding a little extra water if necessary. Meanwhile, heat the butter and oil in a medium frying pan and sauté the leeks gently until soft and golden. Drain excess water from the cooked turnips and potatoes, return to the pot and add the leeks and any buttery pan juices, together with the nutmeg and seasoning. Mash everything together with a little warm milk to make it creamy.

tomato **BOBOTIE**

This recipe, without being hostile to tradition, does differ slightly from the regular. The result is a soft, succulent, slow-baked and very lekker *bobotie. Serve with yellow rice, sambals and atchar.*

1 medium-thick slice crustless white or brown bread

375 ml (1½ cups) milk

30 ml (2 Tbsp) oil

2 medium onions, finely chopped

1 large knob fresh root ginger, peeled, coarsely grated

3 cloves garlic, crushed

45 ml (3 Tbsp) curry powder

5 ml (1 tsp) ground cinnamon

7 ml (1½ tsp) ground cumin

1 kg lean beef mince

1 large carrot, coarsely grated

45 ml (3 Tbsp) fruit chutney

10 ml (2 tsp) sea salt

1 XL free-range egg, beaten

60 ml (4 Tbsp) seedless raisins

250 ml (1 cup) tomato purée

TOPPING

2 XL free-range eggs

a large pinch each of sea salt and turmeric

6 bay leaves

flaked almonds

garam masala

Soak the bread in the milk. Heat the oil in a large pan and fry the onions, ginger and garlic. Add the curry powder and spices. Stir until aromatic, adding a dash of water if necessary to prevent scorching, then add the mince. Toss over low heat until no longer pink. Add the remaining ingredients, including the squeezed-dry bread (reserve the milk). Mix well, then turn into a large, lightly oiled baking dish – about 30 x 20 cm – the meat mixture should be about 3 cm deep. Spread out, then bake at 160 °C for 45 minutes.

For the topping, whisk the eggs with the reserved milk (make it up to 300 ml (1⅕ cups)), salt and turmeric. Pour over the meat. Slip in the bay leaves, scatter with almonds and bake for 45 minutes until set. Sprinkle with garam masala 5 minutes before the end. **Serves 8.**

karoo **BOLOGNESE**

... in which our local big bird is given some foreign treatment and a very long simmer. The result will be a jolly good pasta sauce, not as succulent as when made with beef or lamb or pork, but lean, healthy and a good ethnic alternative.

30 ml (2 Tbsp) oil
15 ml (1 Tbsp) butter
1 large onion, finely chopped
1 stick celery, plus leaves, finely chopped
1 medium carrot, finely diced
500 g ostrich mince
2–3 cloves garlic, crushed
80 ml (⅓ cup) red wine
250 ml (1 cup) tomato purée
500 ml (2 cups) hot beef stock
sea salt, milled black pepper and a little sugar to taste
about 60 ml (4 Tbsp) chopped flat-leaf or curly parsley
2 ml (½ tsp) dried oregano
2 bay leaves
grated or shaved Parmesan cheese

Heat the oil and butter in a large saucepan. Add the vegetables and stir over low heat until beginning to soften. Add the mince and garlic and brown well over medium heat – toss continually to 'loosen' the mince, breaking up any clumps and lumps. Add the wine and simmer until evaporated and only the fragrance lingers, then stir in the remaining ingredients, except the cheese. Reduce the heat to very low and simmer, half-covered, for about 1½ hours, stirring now and then, and adding, if necessary, a little extra stock in order to end up with a thick, rich-looking brown sauce. Remove the bay leaves, ladle the sauce onto servings of spaghetti and top with grated or shaved Parmesan.
Serves 4 generously.

FILLET OF BEEF with a creamy mustard sauce

This makes a rather special meal for four without breaking the budget because you don't have to cater for seconds – unlike a roast, seconds just don't seem polite when it comes to steaks. So: just four tournedos – cut thick, but small – first marinated, then cooked in minutes and finally drizzled with the cream sauce that is much lighter than most, and a snap to prepare.

4 x 100 g slices of fillet
a slick of oil for frying
sea salt and milled black pepper

MARINADE

60 ml (¼ cup) red wine

10 ml (2 tsp) balsamic vinegar

10 ml (2 tsp) olive oil

5 ml (1 tsp) finely chopped rosemary leaves

SAUCE

125 ml (½ cup) reduced-fat cream

30 ml (2 Tbsp) sweet sherry

20 ml (4 tsp) Dijon mustard

1 small clove garlic, crushed

2 spring onions, finely chopped

Mix all the ingredients for the marinade in a small, shallow glass or non-metallic dish, add the steaks and refrigerate for 4–6 hours, turning a few times. Return the steaks to room temperature before cooking. Take them straight out of the marinade without patting them dry, and use a fairly small frying pan – the steaks should not be crowded, but a large pan will reduce the sauce too much. Heat a little oil and brown the steaks on both sides – turn only once and don't have the heat too fierce or the vinegar will scorch. When done to your liking, transfer to a serving platter, season lightly and keep warm while you make the sauce. Stir all the sauce ingredients together, pour into the same pan in which you cooked the steaks, and stir over low heat until smooth and slightly thickened. Mix in any juices that have accumulated under the waiting steaks, drizzle the steaks with the sauce, and serve at once.
Serves 4.

favourite **FAST FILLET**

A recipe for both young, nervous cooks and old, lazy ones because – apart from over-cooking the steak – there are no pitfalls. However, the appeal really lies in the fact that, despite the use of just a few pure, simple ingredients, this does make a rather special quick meal for two steak-lovers, using just one pan.

125 ml (½ cup) beef stock

60 ml (¼ cup) sweet sherry (like OB's)

15 ml (1 Tbsp) light soy sauce

7 ml (1½ tsp) wholegrain mustard

4 large (about 80 g) portabellini mushrooms,
wiped and quartered

2 x beef fillet medallions (about 150 g each)

olive oil

milled black pepper

30 ml (2 Tbsp) cream

30 ml (2 Tbsp) snipped garlic chives

Mix the stock, sherry, soy sauce, mustard and mushrooms and set aside. Brush the steaks with olive oil on both sides, and grind over the pepper. Pan-fry in a slick of extra oil until browned and done to your liking – turn once, without piercing. Don't have the heat too high, as the medallions are thick and will be very rare – unless that is what you want. Set aside, no salt required. To the pan add the mixed ingredients and boil over medium heat, stirring, until the mushrooms have shrunk and the liquid has slightly reduced. (This is not a thick sauce.) Return the steaks to the pan, add the cream and chives, and coat the steaks with the sauce while gently heating through. Serve the medallions with buttered baby potatoes and a salad. **Serves 2**.

FILLET OF BEEF
with port and mushrooms

This is a special occasion, rather extravagant and sensually rich dish, with redcurrant jelly and crème fraîche adding a gourmet touch. It's also very quick to prepare and has to be served immediately, so have everything ready and waiting because once you've started cooking you'll have nearly finished.

30 ml (2 Tbsp) oil

20 ml (4 tsp) butter

4 slices beef fillet of equal size and thickness,
 weighing about 125 g each

sea salt and milled black pepper

6 slim spring onions, chopped

200 g brown mushrooms, wiped and sliced

90 ml (6 Tbsp) port

300 ml (1⅕ cups) hot beef stock

7 ml (1½ tsp) Dijon mustard

10 ml (2 tsp) redcurrant jelly

45–60 ml (3–4 Tbsp) crème fraîche (or thick sour cream)

Heat the oil and butter and, when sizzling, add the steaks. When deeply browned on one side, turn and do the other. If you don't want them rare, reduce the heat to medium and cook just until they're done to your liking, then remove, season lightly and keep warm. Add the onions, mushrooms and port to the pan juices and cook for a few minutes until almost dry, then add the stock, mustard, jelly and crème fraîche. Simmer, uncovered, until slightly reduced and thickened, check the seasoning, and then either nap the waiting steaks with the sauce, or serve it alongside, or make a pool on warmed plates and place the steaks on top. It might sound strange, but simple mashed potatoes are really good with this steak; alternatively, use tiny jacket potatoes and bright vegetables. **Serves 4.**

BEEF STEAKS
with red wine and mushroom sauce

Many people like a little something with their steak and this sauce is for them. Make it while the cooked steaks are settling, then spoon it over, or alongside; the rich red-brown colour and medley of flavours will enhance any cut, but it's specially good with rump or fillet.

oil

6 portions of fillet or 4 medium rump steaks

top-quality soy sauce

1 large leek, thinly shredded

2 cloves garlic, crushed

125 ml (½ cup) red wine

375 ml (1½ cups) hot beef stock

10 ml (2 tsp) tomato paste

200 g brown mushrooms, wiped and chunkily chopped

extra 15 ml (1 Tbsp) soy sauce

20 ml (4 tsp) flour mashed with 20 ml (4 tsp) softened butter

about 5 ml (1 tsp) redcurrant jelly

* No salt has been added to the ingredients as – unless using low-salt soy sauce – extra salt should not be necessary.

Heat a little oil in a large frying pan, brush the steaks on both sides with a little soy sauce (this is optional, but it improves the colour and eliminates the need for salt*) and brown on both sides, turning once only and being careful not to pierce them. (Don't do this over fierce heat or the meat will scorch.) When done to your liking, transfer to a plate and keep warm. Add the leek to the same pan and, when it starts to soften and brown, add the garlic, wine, stock and tomato paste. Allow to bubble over medium heat until slightly reduced and boldly coloured, then add the mushrooms and extra soy sauce. When the mushrooms are softening, stir in the flour-butter paste teaspoon by teaspoon, until the sauce thickens, then add the jelly to gloss it and round out the flavour – if you don't have redcurrant jelly, you could try apple or quince – just a touch of sweetness finishes it off perfectly. Now stir in any juices that have escaped under the waiting steaks, and serve.

Serves 4–6.

LEMONY VEAL escalopes

If you buy escalopes they will need to be flattened with a mallet or rolling pin, so it makes sense to buy schnitzels in the first place. These are easy to find, and schnitzel is simply the Austrian word for a very thin escalope (or scallopine), so it boils down to the same thing really – a thin slice of veal, ready to be used in this luscious, lemony, quick dish. If doubling up, you'll need a jumbo frying pan – otherwise use two pans to avoid crowding.

30 ml (2 Tbsp) flour

4 fresh young sage leaves, finely chopped

4 veal schnitzels (about 270 g total weight)

30 ml (2 Tbsp) olive oil

a pat of butter

sea salt to taste

60 ml (¼ cup) white vermouth

175 ml (⅔ cup) chicken stock

7 ml (1½ tsp) rinsed, chopped capers

30 ml (2 Tbsp) finely chopped fresh flat-leaf parsley

2 ml (½ tsp) very finely grated lemon rind

10 ml (2 tsp) butter

Mix the flour and sage and use to coat both sides of the veal. Heat the oil and butter in a frying pan wide enough to take the schnitzels in a single layer. Fry quickly on both sides until just cooked and golden brown, then transfer to a plate and season. Reduce the heat and pour the vermouth into the pan. Reduce by half, then add the stock, capers, parsley and lemon rind, all mixed together. Simmer for 2–3 minutes while enjoying the lovely lemony whiff, then swirl in the butter and return the veal just to heat through – don't overcook, as the schnitzels will toughen. Serve at once with the juices poured over, and lemon wedges for squeezing. **Serves 4 modestly.**

CASSEROLE OF VEAL with brinjals and olives

Not unlike Osso Buco, but with chunky Mediterranean vegetables adding their individual character and flavour.

1 kg veal shin, in 2 cm thick slices (10–12 slices)
seasoned flour
olive oil
1 x 400 g can whole tomatoes, chopped, plus juice
2 medium (500 g) aubergines (brinjals),
cubed and dégorged
3 sticks celery, chopped
12 pickling onions, peeled
15 ml (1 Tbsp) tomato paste
7 ml (1½ tsp) dried tarragon
125 ml (½ cup) white wine
250 ml (1 cup) chicken stock
5 ml (1 tsp) sea salt
10 ml (2 tsp) sugar
6 cloves garlic, peeled
3 bay leaves
black olives (as many as you like)
chopped fresh tarragon or flat-leaf parsley to garnish

Nick the edges of the veal slices, roll in seasoned flour, and brown on both sides in a little olive oil in a frying pan – do this in batches – then arrange in a large baking dish in a single layer. Add the remaining ingredients, except the olives and garnish, to the pan, stir to mix, then cover and simmer for 10 minutes. Pour the sauce over the veal, pushing the onions in between the slices, then cover securely with a lid, or a sheet of greaseproof paper and then one of foil, and bake at 160 °C for 1½ hours, by which time the veal should be butter-soft, the vegetables cooked, and the sauce rich and thick. Stir in the olives and, if necessary, a little extra stock and return to the oven, uncovered, until bubbling. Remove and discard the bay leaves and sprinkle with the tarragon or parsley. **Serves 6.**

BUFFALO LAMB
with peppadews

You may wonder about the word 'buffalo' in a recipe without buffalo, but the word also features in a chicken dish – also without buffalo, but with a signature tomatoey/mustardy/sweetish sauce. I can't imagine what a buffalo has to do with it, but I thought if chicken can respond to it, so can lamb. You will need a really large, wide pan.

30 ml (2 Tbsp) oil and a pat of butter

6 lamb chump chops (about 600 g), trimmed of rind
and excess fat

a little sea salt and milled black pepper

1 large onion, sliced into thin rings

2 medium carrots, diced

30 ml (2 Tbsp) flour

125 ml (½ cup) tomato purée

125 ml (½ cup) red wine

250 ml (1 cup) beef stock

10 ml (2 tsp) Worcestershire sauce

30 ml (2 Tbsp) chutney

15 ml (1 Tbsp) wholegrain mustard

2–3 bay leaves

15 ml (1 Tbsp) soft brown sugar

5 ml (1 tsp) mixed dried herbs

a jar of mild sweet piquanté peppers (Peppadews)

a handful of chopped fresh flat-leaf parsley or coriander

Heat the oil and butter, brown both sides of the chops, set aside, and season. Add the onion and carrots to the pan and, when softening, sprinkle in the flour. When absorbed, add the remaining ingredients, except the Peppadews and parsley, stir to mix, then return the lamb to the pan. Cover and simmer gently over very low heat, stirring occasionally, for 1 hour, turning once, and adding a little extra stock only if necessary. When the chops are very tender and the sauce bright and medium-thick, reach for the jar of Peppadews and rinse and chop enough to provide 60–75 ml (4–5 Tbsp). Stir them into the sauce, heat for 10 minutes, remove the bay leaves, then swirl in the parsley or coriander. Serve on rice or, if the pan is big enough, add baby potatoes to cook through just before the chops are tender. **Serves 4–6, with a green veg.**

SAUCY LAMB KNUCKLES
with butternut and chickpeas

The dish is quite different from a bredie, and makes the most of a modest amount of lamb. A side dish of braised brinjals and peppers would round it off nicely, or simply a good spinach salad and brown rice, or baby potatoes. A dollop of Greek yoghurt on the side is an indulgent but super option.

a little oil

950 g–1 kg free-range Karoo lamb knuckles, sliced

sea salt to taste

2 medium onions, finely chopped

3–4 cloves garlic, crushed

10 ml (2 tsp) each ground cumin and coriander

30 ml (2 Tbsp) flour

250 ml (1 cup) hot, seasoned beef stock

125 ml (½ cup) red wine

1 x 410 g can chopped, peeled tomatoes (as opposed to whole peeled tomatoes, if possible)

15 ml (1 Tbsp) tomato paste

1 medium butternut, peeled and diced (400 g prepared weight)

15 ml (1 Tbsp) honey

2 fat sticks cinnamon

4 bay leaves

1 x 410 g can chickpeas, drained and rinsed

chopped fresh coriander leaves for topping

Heat the oil in a large frying pan and brown the lamb well. Remove to a baking dish (30 x 24 x 6 cm is dead right) – the knuckles should not be crowded as the sauce is bulky. Season. Add the onions, garlic and spices to the pan drippings and toss for 1–2 minutes (if dry, add a dash of water). Add the flour, stir until absorbed, then slowly stir in the stock, wine and tomatoes. When thickening, add the remaining ingredients, except the chickpeas and coriander. Bring to the boil, then mix into the lamb. Cover with a lid, or greaseproof paper and then foil, and bake at 160 °C for 1¼ hours. Remove the bay leaves and cinnamon. Add the chickpeas, cover again and bake for 30 minutes; the lamb should be tender and the sauce thick and plentiful. Sprinkle with coriander.

Serves 5–6.

SPICY LAMB, butter bean and cauli curry

Call it old-fashioned, but this is just the stuff that memories are made of – warming, comforting food without any disconcerting frills. The only possible hiccup is the need for an exceptionally wide saucepan so that the ingredients don't lie on top of each other, but can wallow in the lovely sauce. Otherwise it's hassle-free.

8 (about 800 g) lamb chump chops (not braai chops, but
   those meaty little slabs with a tiny bone in the centre)
30 ml (2 Tbsp) oil
1 large onion, sliced into thin rings
1 small red chilli, seeded and chopped
15 ml (1 Tbsp) curry powder
5 ml (1 tsp) ground cumin
2 ml (½ tsp) each ground cinnamon and turmeric
30 ml (2 Tbsp) flour
375 ml (1½ cups) hot beef stock
150 ml (⅗ cup) tomato purée
2 cloves garlic, crushed
sea salt and a little sugar
1 x 410 g can butter beans, rinsed and drained
200 g small cauliflower florets
a generous sprinkling of fresh coriander leaves

Slice the chops in half. Heat the oil gently in that very large pan. Add the onion, chilli and spices, toss briefly until smelling gorgeous, then add the lamb and brown on both sides. If the spices start to scorch, add a dribble of water, but do brown the lamb well. Reduce the heat to very low and sprinkle in the flour. Toss, and when the flour has been absorbed, slowly add the stock, tomato purée, garlic, salt and sugar. Cover, and simmer over very low heat for 1 hour, stirring from time to time. Mix in the butter beans and cauliflower – there should be no need to add extra liquid, as the slow simmer should have resulted in a medium-thick, plentiful sauce. Cover and simmer for 20 minutes to cook the cauliflower, then check the seasoning. If it is tart, add a dribble of honey, it does wonders; and if time allows, and you are using a non-reactive pan, allow the curry to cool down a bit. Reheat just before serving, sprinkle with the coriander, and serve from the pan with yellow rice and chutney. **Serves 4–6.**

CASSEROLE OF LAMB with mushrooms and butter beans

An earthy stew, brimming with tender nuggets of lamb and vegetables in a thick, herby gravy.
Preparation is quick, the baking very slow, and interference from the cook virtually nil,
yet the result is simply delicious.

1.1 kg lamb knuckles (20–24), sliced 3–4 cm thick*
seasoned flour
oil
4 cloves garlic, chopped
2 large onions, coarsely chopped
3 medium carrots, sliced
5 ml (1 tsp) each dried thyme and oregano
125 ml (½ cup) red wine
200 ml (⅘ cup) beef stock
200 ml (⅘ cup) tomato purée
125 ml (½ cup) parsley tufts
10 ml (2 tsp) Worcestershire sauce
5 ml (1 tsp) sea salt
10 ml (2 tsp) soft brown sugar
200 g brown mushrooms, wiped and chopped
4 bay leaves
1 x 410 g can butter beans, drained and rinsed

Roll the knuckles in the seasoned flour or shake up in a bag – the easiest way. Brown in batches on both sides in a little oil, then transfer to a large baking dish – 20 x 30 cm is perfect. Place the remaining ingredients, except the mushrooms, bay leaves and beans, in a processor fitted with the metal blade and pulse until the vegetables are finely chopped. Mix with the mushrooms, then spread the mixture over the knuckles. Tuck in the bay leaves and cover securely with a lid, or a sheet of greaseproof paper and then one of foil. Bake at 160 °C for 1 hour, then turn and toss the knuckles – the juices will have drawn, but the meat will not yet be tender and the flavour of the sauce will not have mellowed. Cover as before and bake for a further 1 hour, then add the beans and bake, uncovered, for about 15 minutes or until the sauce has thickened sufficiently. Remove and discard the bay leaves and serve piping hot.
Serves 6.

* Do not substitute 'stewing' lamb as it is too fatty.

valentine's **LAMB**

In earlier times, Valentine's Day was certainly not celebrated with sparkling wine and oysters and heart-shaped chocolate mousses. If a young lady wanted to impress her young man with a home-cooked meal, she would definitely have cooked the favourite: lamb. The men loved roast lamb (and probably still do), but to present a suitor with a whole leg would be plain stupid. It would take him half the night to eat, and leave no time for other things.

1 kg (half a leg, no shank bone) free-range Karoo lamb
a little vinegar
250 ml (1 cup) buttermilk
4 large sprigs fresh rosemary, lightly crushed
30 ml (2 Tbsp) seasoned flour
7 ml (1½ tsp) dried oregano
45 ml (3 Tbsp) olive oil
1 onion, finely chopped
a few bay leaves
4 large cloves garlic, unpeeled
250 ml (1 cup) water
dry red wine
8 large brown mushrooms, wiped, left whole

Wipe the leg with vinegar, place in a dish suitable for marinating, pour over the buttermilk and rub to coat it. Add the rosemary and refrigerate for 20–24 hours.

To roast, rinse off all the buttermilk. Dry the leg well, then rub all over with the seasoned flour and oregano. Brown gently in the heated oil in a small frying pan. Place the onion, bay leaves, garlic and water in a non-reactive baking dish, add the lamb and pour over the drippings from the pan. Roast, uncovered, at 160 °C for 1 hour, baste and add a dash (about 60 ml (¼ cup)) of red wine, then continue to bake until the aroma calls you back to the kitchen – another hour. Arrange the mushrooms round the leg, add another swig of wine, roast a further 15 minutes, then switch off the oven and leave for 15 minutes before carving. Serve with the delicious juices spooned over the meat and mushrooms, and 2 cloves garlic each for squeezing – the flesh will be subtle and mellowed; in any case you're both eating it! **Serves 2 with leftovers.**

BRAISED LAMB STEAKS with wine and herbs

The 'proper' meat to use here would be stewing mutton, which requires long, slow cooking, but there's nothing wrong with treating steaks in the same way. Serve with sprouts and spuds.

4 lamb steaks (about 600 g)
30 ml (2 Tbsp) oil and a nut of butter
1 large onion, finely chopped
30 ml (2 Tbsp) red wine
a pinch of sugar
2 leeks, thinly sliced
4 slender carrots, diced
30 ml (2 Tbsp) flour
1 sprig of fresh rosemary and 4 sprigs of fresh thyme
extra 125 ml (½ cup) red wine
250 ml (1 cup) hot beef stock
5 ml (1 tsp) Worcestershire sauce
2 bay leaves
a little sea salt
125 g brown mushrooms, wiped and sliced
20 ml (4 tsp) redcurrant jelly

Pull off the thin outer rind from each steak, then slice each into four. Heat the oil and butter in a large, deep saucepan (unless you have a very large, deep frying pan). Brown the lamb well on each side, then remove from the pan. Add the onion, the 30 ml (2 Tbsp) red wine and the sugar to the pan, and cook until the wine has evaporated and the onion has started to brown. Add the leeks and carrots (if there's no more fat left, add a dash of water to prevent burning). Stir for a few minutes, then return the meat to the pan, sprinkle with the flour and, when that's absorbed, add the herbs, extra red wine, stock, Worcestershire sauce, bay leaves and salt. Cover securely and simmer over very low heat for 1 hour, shaking the pan (or giving the contents a gentle stir) occasionally; the meat should be tender and the gravy thickened. Remove the bay leaves and herb stalks and add the mushrooms. Cover again and simmer for 15 minutes while they release their juices, then stir in the jelly and allow to melt. If time allows, cool the stew, then reheat gently, for the finest flavour. **Makes 4 generous servings.**

simmered, savoury **LAMB LOIN CHOPS**

When I see loin chops I can think of nothing but red wine, rosemary and mushrooms. There has to be a reason –
and I think it is this: the marriage is so perfect, the balance of flavours so impeccable, why follow a different route?

1–2 cloves garlic

12 lamb loin chops (1–1.2 kg), rind and excess fat removed

60 ml (¼ cup) oil and a pat of butter

sea salt and milled black pepper

4 large leeks, shredded

180 ml (¾ cup) tomato purée

150 ml (⅗ cup) red wine

500 ml (2 cups) beef stock*

2 small sprigs fresh rosemary, bruised

4 sprigs fresh oregano, bruised

4 bay leaves

15 ml (1 Tbsp) soft brown sugar

300 g mixed mushrooms, wiped and coarsely chopped**

1 ml (¼ tsp) ground cinnamon

10 ml (2 tsp) redcurrant, apple or quince jelly

Halve the cloves of garlic and rub well into the chops on both sides. Heat the oil and butter in a very large, deep frying pan and add the chops, tail ends curled round, and brown on both sides. When you get that lovely aroma, remove the chops, season lightly and set aside. Soften the leeks in the pan drippings, then add the remaining ingredients up to, and including, the sugar. Bring to simmering point, stirring, then return the lamb to the pan and add the mushrooms and cinnamon. Reduce the heat, cover and simmer very gently for about 30 minutes, turning once.
By this time the chops should be really tender, so transfer them to a serving dish, remove the rosemary and oregano from the sauce and boil rapidly for a few minutes to reduce. Swirl in the jelly to gloss and after a minute or so pour over the chops and serve.
Serves 6.

* I use Marmite rather than a cube – it makes a dark, flavoursome stock.
** The choice is flexible – I use a mix of brown, button and baby button.

braised LEG OF LAMB

This dish is a cook's dream – simply left to languish in the oven for hours along with plenty of wine, stock, vegetables and other things, it emerges butter-soft and afloat with flavour. Add potatoes before the end, and bake butternut seeing the oven is on. Two imperatives – you'll need a heavy, lidded roaster that can be used on the stove and in the oven – and a good red wine.

1.5 kg leg of lamb (without the shank bone)
vinegar
lots of garlic, slivered
15 ml (1 Tbsp) flour mixed with 5 ml (1 tsp) sea salt
about 30 ml (2 Tbsp) oil (and a dab of butter for flavour)
2 large onions, chopped
2 large carrots, diced
1 stick celery, plus leaves, chopped
2 ml (½ tsp) dried oregano
200 ml (⅘ cup) red wine (preferably claret)
200 ml (⅘ cup) hot beef stock
2–3 x 10 cm sprigs of fresh rosemary
15 ml (1 Tbsp) tomato paste
15 ml (1 Tbsp) soft brown sugar
10 ml (2 tsp) Worcestershire sauce
3 bay leaves

Wipe the leg with vinegar, jab little slits here and there, insert the garlic, and rub all over with the seasoned flour. Heat the oil and butter in the roaster (no rack needed with this recipe), brown the lamb, then remove. Add the vegetables and oregano to the drippings and sweat briefly over low heat. Return the meat to the roaster, add the remaining ingredients, baste the leg, then place in the oven at 160 °C for 1½ hours. Turn the leg, cover again, and bake for a further 1 hour (slip potatoes round the meat, if using). Remove to a warm platter to rest – switch off the oven and leave the lamb there while you make the gravy. Either reduce it on the stove, which can be dodgy because it concentrates the flavours, which may be quite concentrated already, or break the rules and use cornflour slaked with a little red wine, boil up, and when the consistency is right, remove the bay leaves. Pour a little over the lamb, and serve the rest separately. **Serves 6.**

PORK CHOPS with cider, apple and sage

Cider with pork is a natural marriage of flavours. Add some apples, fresh sage and a few other bits and bobs,
give it all a slow-bake, and out comes a homely but very good casserole to serve with cabbage and mash.
It is important to use fresh, not dried sage.

15 ml (1 Tbsp) oil and a dab of butter

1 really large onion, sliced into thin rings

4 large pork leg chops (650–700 g), 2–2.5 cm thick,
   rind and excess fat removed

a little sea salt and ground cinnamon

30 ml (2 Tbsp) flour

125 ml (½ cup) hot, seasoned chicken stock

250 ml (1 cup) extra-dry cider

about 6 fresh sage leaves, roughly torn

10 ml (2 tsp) Dijon mustard

a few rinsed and chopped capers (optional)

15 ml (1 Tbsp) light honey

2 medium dessert apples (not Grannies),
   peeled and chopped

Heat the oil and butter in a wide frying pan. Add
the onion and cook until just beginning to colour
(a pinch of sugar helps). Spread the onions over the
base of a baking dish big enough to take the chops
in a single layer, and deep enough to hold the sauce.
In the pan, fry the chops on both sides; keep the heat
to medium (high heat toughens pork chops) and
remove when they're lightly toasted in colour.
Place on top of the onions and sprinkle with salt
and cinnamon. Stir the flour into the pan drippings
(if there aren't any, add a spoon of oil or butter)
and, when it starts to colour, add the stock and cider.
Bring to the boil, stirring vigorously to smooth out
any lumps, then remove from the heat. Add the
remaining ingredients and slowly pour over the
chops, tucking the diced apples wherever there's
room in between. Cover the dish with greaseproof
paper and then foil, and bake just below the centre
of the oven at 160 °C for 1½ hours, then turn the
chops. Re-cover, and bake for a further 30 minutes,
or until the chops are very tender in a savoury gravy,
remembering that they're thick, and have little bone
to conduct the heat, so they might take longer than
you'd expect. **Serves 4.**

orange **PORK CHOPS**

Bathed in a savoury orange sauce and then slow-baked until meltingly tender, this dish is hassle free, has lots of character, and is quite voluptuously satisfying. Simple accompaniments like mash and broccoli team up perfectly with these bright, succulent chops.

a dash of oil

6 large pork loin chops (about 1 kg), without rind or excess fat

a little sea salt

250 ml (1 cup) fresh orange juice

30 ml (2 Tbsp) soy sauce

30 ml (2 Tbsp) smooth chutney

2 ml (½ tsp) ground cinnamon

a small knob of fresh root ginger, peeled and coarsely grated

5 ml (1 tsp) very finely grated orange rind

10 ml (2 tsp) runny honey

60 ml (4 Tbsp) seedless raisins

30 ml (2 Tbsp) flour

verjuice (optional)

Heat the oil in a large frying pan, add the chops and seal quickly on both sides – do not brown. Transfer to a baking dish to fit fairly closely, and season lightly. Quickly mix the orange juice with the rest of the ingredients, except the flour and the verjuice. Add the flour to the pan drippings and, when absorbed, add the orange juice mixture. Stir while it comes to the boil, then pour over the chops. Cover securely with a sheet of greaseproof paper and then one of foil, and bake at 160 °C for 1 hour. Turn the chops, cover again, and bake for a further 15 minutes, by which time they should be wonderfully tender in a toffee-coloured sauce. Taste and, if too sweet for your liking, add a dash of verjuice. **Serves 6**.

PASTA

ROBUST TOMATO SAUCE
with herbs

A simple tomato sauce is the starting point for hundreds of pasta dishes and anyone who loves pasta won't need a recipe for the basic mix of tomatoes, onion, garlic, basil and olive oil. The following recipe, however, takes this mix a step further, with the addition of extra herbs and Italian white beans. Canned tomatoes and dried herbs are often used in these sauces, but fresh ingredients have a very special appeal. I also toss in a few mushrooms because I think they enhance almost everything, and although the result is still a basic tomato sauce, it has a lot more personality and flavour than the simpler version.

45 ml (3 Tbsp) olive oil
1 large onion, finely chopped
3 cloves garlic, crushed
1 small green pepper, seeded, ribs removed, and chopped
500 g ripe, juicy tomatoes, skinned and finely chopped
10 ml (2 tsp) tomato paste
15 ml (1 Tbsp) fresh oregano leaves
15 ml (1 Tbsp) fresh thyme leaves
2 bay leaves
a few tufts of parsley
sea salt, milled black pepper and a pinch of sugar
60 ml (¼ cup) red wine
1 x 400 g can cannellini beans, drained and rinsed*
a few fresh basil leaves, shredded
100 g brown mushrooms, wiped and sliced
slivered black olives
a pat of butter
grated Parmesan or pecorino cheese for sprinkling

Heat the oil in a large pan and sauté the onion, garlic and green pepper. Add the tomatoes, tomato paste, herbs (except basil), seasoning and wine. Cover and simmer over very low heat for 30–40 minutes. Stir occasionally and mash up the tomatoes with a wooden spoon. (The pan should be covered or the sauce will thicken too much, and the beans will thicken it even further.) Mix in the beans, basil, mushrooms, olives and butter and simmer, covered, for a further 15 minutes – you will probably need to add a little water or stock to keep it succulent. It's the long, gentle simmer that's important here to mellow the flavours – quick tomato sauces can be very tart. Serve on fettucine and pass the cheese. **Serves 4 very generously.**

*These are white kidney beans, larger than haricots, smaller than butter beans.

SMOKED SALMON PASTA with mushrooms and cream

I'm not a fan of smoked foods, but salmon is my downfall. Eat it with pasta in a restaurant, however, and it is often so richly extravagant one would not consider making it at home – not often, anyway. Now this recipe was devised with an eye to scaling the whole lot down – mushrooms to pad it out and milk and cornflour (I blush, I blush) to dilute the cream – and it really works rather well despite the liberties taken.

500 g button mushrooms, wiped and thinly sliced

6–8 spring onions, chopped

250 ml (1 cup) cream

250 ml (1 cup) milk

125 ml (½ cup) off-dry white wine

30 ml (2 Tbsp) tomato paste

a little sea salt

30 ml (2 Tbsp) cornflour

about 320 g smoked salmon, sliced into thin strips

400 g pasta screws

Put the mushrooms and spring onions into a large saucepan. In a separate bowl, stir together the cream, milk, wine, tomato paste, salt and cornflour until smooth, then mix into the mushrooms. Bring to the boil, then simmer, covered, over low heat for about 10 minutes until thick and creamy. Stir in the salmon and heat through.

Cook the pasta while the sauce is simmering, then drain and place in a large, heated serving dish. Pour the sauce over the top, toss until combined, and serve immediately with a dressed salad, passing a pepper mill at the table. **Serves 6.**

mushroom and spinach **NOODLE BAKE**

A layered pasta casserole is a fine example of comfort food, and this dish, with its succulent mix of vegetables, noodles and a blanket of sauce has a lot more style than macaroni cheese. As it can be completely assembled in advance, and sits well alongside a salad and bread, it offers a happy choice for informal entertaining.

30 ml (2 Tbsp) olive oil

1 large onion, finely chopped

2–3 cloves garlic, crushed

1 small or ½ large green pepper, seeded, ribs removed, and diced

250 g brown mushrooms, wiped and sliced

2 ml (½ tsp) dried mixed herbs

250 g ripe tomatoes, skinned and chopped

15 ml (1 Tbsp) tomato paste

5 ml (1 tsp) each sea salt and sugar

milled black pepper

2 bay leaves

60 ml (¼ cup) red wine

500 ml (2 cups) shredded baby spinach

200 g spinach tagliatelle

freshly grated nutmeg and Parmesan cheese for topping

CHEESE SAUCE

30 ml (2 Tbsp) oil and a nut of butter

45 ml (3 Tbsp) flour

5 ml (1 tsp) mustard powder

500 ml (2 cups) warmed full-cream or low-fat milk

100 g Cheddar cheese, grated

sea salt and white pepper

Heat the oil in a large frying pan. Add the onion, garlic and green pepper, toss until softening, then add the mushrooms and herbs. Reduce the heat and toss until aromatic, then add the remaining ingredients, except the spinach, pasta and topping. Cover and simmer, stirring off and on to mash up the tomatoes. Keep the heat very low to retain succulence – 15 minutes should do it. Just before it comes off the heat, remove the bay leaves, stir in the spinach and allow it to wilt. While the sauce is simmering, cook the pasta.

Make a white sauce as usual, adding the cheese and seasoning last. Lightly oil a baking dish, 28 x 18 x 6 cm. Cover the base with half the vegetable sauce and top with half the noodles. Repeat the layers, then pour the cheese sauce over the top. Sprinkle with nutmeg, then Parmesan, and bake at 180 °C for 35 minutes. Leave to settle for 10 minutes before serving. **Serves 6.**

SAUCY PASTA in a bowl

There are times when you have a craving for pasta but you have done pasta with pesto, pasta with olives, pasta with garlic and oil and herbs so often that you can taste everything in your head without going near the kitchen. There are times when you just want to put everything into a pot and go away. That's when this fuss-free dish comes in useful. It's not a mean or a lean meal – it can't be, seeing it requires pecorino and pine nuts – but the chunky vegetable sauce is a simple doddle.

500 g brown mushrooms, wiped and chunkily chopped
2 onions, finely chopped
4 cloves garlic, crushed
400 g courgettes (baby marrows), pared and diced
1 large red pepper, seeded, ribs removed, and chopped
250 ml (1 cup) red wine
400 ml (1⅗ cups) vegetable or chicken stock
10 ml (2 tsp) dried oregano
5 ml (1 tsp) sea salt
30 ml (2 Tbsp) each flour and softened butter
250 g pasta screws, cooked at the last minute
grated or shaved pecorino, toasted pine nuts and
**   olive oil to accompany**

Put the mushrooms, onions, garlic, courgettes, red pepper, wine, stock, oregano and salt into a large saucepan. Bring to the boil, then reduce the heat immediately, stir to mix, then cover and simmer very gently for about 30 minutes until the vegetables are soft and mingled into a succulent, dark sauce. Mash the flour and butter to a paste and add it in small pats, stirring – you might not need all of it, it depends on how much of the liquid has simmered away – use just enough to thicken the sauce to coat the pasta. Serve in deep bowls – first the pasta, then a ladleful of sauce, with the cheese, nuts and olive oil passed separately. The end result is hugely satisfying, so no bread required, but an undressed green salad with rocket is good. **Serves 6.**

pasta **STROGANOFF**

Also known as Slimmer's Stroganoff because the sour cream used in traditional stroganoff has been left out, but it's actually nowhere near a slimming dish – what mix of fried steak in a thick, creamy gravy can possibly be? Nevertheless, it has its virtues: it stretches a little fillet to feed a lot, it's a change from bolognaise, and the flavour is good. Although stroganoff is often served on fluffy rice, tagliatelle or fettucine is used here. Add a big green salad, and you have a no-frills, pasta party dish, and a welcome change from bolognaise.

600 g fillet of beef
20 ml (4 tsp) Worcestershire sauce
3–4 cloves garlic, crushed
2 ml (½ tsp) dried thyme, crushed
30 ml (2 Tbsp) oil
250 g brown mushrooms, wiped and sliced
1 large bunch of spring onions, chopped
500 ml (2 cups) low-fat milk
30 ml (2 Tbsp) tomato paste
25 ml (5 tsp) soy sauce
a pinch each of sea salt and sugar
20 ml (4 tsp) cornflour
45 ml (3 Tbsp) medium-dry sherry

Slice the beef across the grain into wafer-thin strips – most easily done if the beef is semi-frozen. Place in a large, shallow dish, add the Worcestershire sauce, garlic and thyme, toss to mix, then cover loosely and leave to stand for 45 minutes.
Heat the oil in a large frying pan and stir-fry the steak briefly, until just browned, tossing all the time. Add the mushrooms and spring onions, and keep tossing over medium heat until softening, then turn the heat to very low and add the milk, tomato paste, soy sauce, salt and sugar. Stir to mix, then cover and simmer very gently for 4–5 minutes. Mix the cornflour with the sherry, stir into the pan and allow to boil up, stirring, until the sauce has smoothed out and thickened. **Serves 6**.

the simplest **VEGETABLE PASTA**

When you read the recipe you'll see how easy it is, and when you taste it you'll know that it's one you'll turn to often: a couple of ingredients, a couple of minutes, and there you have a salubrious tangle of spinach fettucine with in-and-out-of-the-pan vegetables. Lots of flavour, little effort, and profoundly useful.

30 ml (2 Tbsp) olive oil

2 cloves garlic, crushed

6 spring onions, chopped

250 g large white mushrooms, wiped and sliced

1 red pepper, seeded, ribs removed, and julienned

120 g baby spinach, roughly torn

2 ml (½ tsp) freshly grated nutmeg

30 ml (2 Tbsp) white vermouth

200 g spinach fettucine, cooked and drained

a few fresh basil leaves, torn

a little sea salt

45 ml (3 Tbsp) butter

45 ml (3 Tbsp) grated Parmesan or pecorino cheese

Mix the oil, all the vegetables, the nutmeg and vermouth in a large saucepan. Heat, and toss for a few minutes, until just beginning to wilt. Add the fettucine, and toss together lightly, adding the basil, salt, butter and cheese. Simply super served with extra grated cheese, a flat bread topped with tomatoes and olives, and a green salad – undressed, but pass some good olive oil for those who want it. **Serves 4.**

PESTO PASTA with roasted tomatoes and butternut

This pasta dish is a real treat. Only a few ingredients required, and little effort involved, but the result is brilliantly flavoured, colourful, and quite different from most pasta and veg combinations. Do use Roma tomatoes – a variation of plum tomato, they are deep red in colour and the size and shape of a hen's egg.

500 g Roma tomatoes, quartered
500 g peeled and cubed butternut (prepared weight)
45 ml (3 Tbsp) olive oil
5 ml (1 tsp) dried oregano
5 ml (1 tsp) sea salt
a sprinkling of light brown sugar
200–250 g fusilli tricolore or pasta screws
about 100 ml (⅖ cup) walnut pesto, or to taste*
shaved pecorino or Parmesan cheese and toasted pine nuts for serving

Place the tomatoes and butternut in a baking dish large enough to hold them in a single layer – 32 x 25 x 6 cm is just right. Moisten them with the olive oil, and sprinkle with the oregano, salt and sugar. Roast at 200 °C for about 30 minutes – the tomatoes should be wrinkled and the butternut soft. Meanwhile, cook the pasta, drain well, mix in the pesto, then tip into the roasted vegetables in the baking dish and combine everything gently. Top each serving with shaved pecorino cheese and roasted pine nuts, and if you pass a flat bread and some olive oil for dipping, you'll have a hugely satisfying meal. I also add a bowl of undressed salad leaves – the crunchy freshness is welcome, as the rest of the meal is very generous with oil.
Serves 4–6, depending on the amount of pasta and pesto you wish to use.

* See page 28, or use your favourite pesto.

PASTA PARTY SALAD
with roasted vegetables

A magnificent party salad: a medley of vegetables, marinated in oil with fresh herbs, roasted until succulent, then tossed with pasta. It can be made a day ahead and refrigerated. Serve mounded on a platter, dotted with black olives and crumbled feta, with a warm flat bread on the side.

500 g aubergines (brinjals), cubed and dégorged

3 large yellow peppers (300 g), seeded, ribs removed, and sliced

500 g courgettes (baby marrows), pared and julienned

250–300 g brown mushrooms, wiped and chunkily chopped

2–4 slender leeks, wiped and sliced into 4 cm pieces

100 ml (⅖ cup) each olive and canola or sunflower oil

3 cloves garlic, crushed

45 ml (3 Tbsp) fresh lemon juice

5 ml (1 tsp) each sea salt and sugar

4 large sprigs each fresh rosemary, thyme and marjoram

250 g broccoli florets

375 ml (1½ cups) elbow macaroni

Place the aubergines, yellow peppers, courgettes, mushrooms and leeks in a very large porcelain baking dish, about 27 x 22 x 7 cm. Mix the oils, garlic, lemon juice, salt and sugar and pour over. Tuck in the herbs and toss to mix everything together, then cover and leave to stand for about 2 hours, tossing when you think of it. Roast, uncovered, at 220 °C for 20 minutes. Remove from the oven, toss to mix, then reduce the temperature to 180 °C and bake for a further 20 minutes or until the vegetables are juicy and tender. Discard the stalks of the herbs – most of the leaves will have fallen off, adding their flavour to the juices. Steam the broccoli until just tender, and drain. Cook the pasta, then drain. Mix these with the vegetables and set aside to cool. Garnish as suggested above and serve at room temperature, or refrigerate (in glass) overnight, then garnish just before serving. **Serves 8–10.**

FAST FUSILLI
with rocket and roasted garlic

... and broccoli and cherry tomatoes – all cooked in one pot. This is a really good answer to the quest for fast food that manages to be both tasty and trendy. If you roast the garlic in the oven at the same time that you're heating the ciabatta and at the same time that you're cooking the pasta, supper will be ready in under 30 minutes.

250–275 g fusilli or farfalle

300 g broccoli florets, halved

400 g cherry tomatoes, slit on one side,
but not cut through

a large handful each of rocket and baby spinach leaves,
rinsed and dried

about 15 ml (1 Tbsp) basil pesto

60 ml (4 Tbsp) olive oil

60 ml (4 Tbsp) grated Parmesan or pecorino cheese

sea salt if necessary

12–16 plump cloves garlic, unpeeled

shaved Parmesan cheese to serve

Cook the pasta as usual, in a large, deep saucepan with lots of water, a little salt and a dash of oil. Shortly before it's done *al dente*, drop in the broccoli and tomatoes, return to the boil and, after a few minutes, when the broccoli looks tender, drain in a colander and tip everything into a large, warmed serving dish. Quickly mix in the rocket, spinach, pesto, olive oil and cheese. Check seasoning and serve with the garlic (see below) and hot, crusty Italian bread and shaved Parmesan.
Serves 4 modestly.

ROASTED GARLIC

Place the separated cloves (unpeeled, but loose, papery skin removed) in a small ovenproof dish. Add a little olive oil, toss to coat and then roast at 200 °C for about 25 minutes until browning and smelling good. Pass them around and allow diners to squeeze the smooth, mellow pulp into their pasta.

PASTA PUTTANESCA SALAD with basil oil

This zesty pasta dish is usually served hot, but it also makes a vibrant salad. The sauce – plenty of tomatoes, with anchovies, chillies and olives – is rather different from most pasta sauces, while the dark, dense basil oil is a personal twist that adds both richness and flavour.

30 ml (2 Tbsp) olive oil

1 x 50 g can flat fillets of anchovied sardines, drained and briefly soaked in milk

1 bunch of spring onions or 6 baby leeks, sliced

2 cloves garlic, crushed

2 x 400 g cans chopped tomatoes in juice

12 black olives, stoned and slivered

1–2 fresh chillies, seeded and chopped

1 large yellow pepper, seeded, ribs removed, and thinly sliced

a handful of fresh flat-leaf parsley

a little sea salt and about 10 ml (2 tsp) sugar*

250 g fusilli tricolore

BASIL OIL

30 g fresh basil leaves, washed, dried

250 ml (1 cup) oil

a small pinch each of sugar and salt

Heat the olive oil with the oil from the anchovies in a wide frying pan. Add the spring onions and garlic and stir for a minute. Add the remaining ingredients, except the pasta. Simmer over low heat, uncovered, stirring until thickened. Taste. If not hot enough, add a sprinkling of crushed dried chillies. Simmer for 10 minutes more. Cook the pasta, then turn into a serving dish. Add the sauce, toss to combine, then leave to cool – the sauce will gradually be absorbed. Cover and leave for up to 2 hours or refrigerate overnight in a covered glass bowl.

Blend all the basil oil ingredients well. Pass round in a jug to be trickled (sparingly) over each serving. (Can also be refrigerated overnight.) You could also pass a bowl of grated pecorino. **Serves 6.**

*This may seem like a lot of sugar, but canned tomatoes are tart and need long simmering to mellow them. As the cooking time in this recipe is short, you will need a little extra sweetness.

PASTA, BEAN AND ROCKET SALAD with pine nuts

A bright, succulent mixture of colourful fusilli tossed up with stir-fried vegetables; added substance comes from the borlotti beans, and lots of flavour from the rocket, cheese and nuts. Super for lunch with a hunk of flat bread.

75 ml (5 Tbsp) olive oil
4–6 spring onions, chopped
2 cloves garlic, crushed
1 red pepper, seeded, ribs removed, and julienned
125 g courgettes (baby marrows), pared and julienned
125–250 g button mushrooms, wiped and chunkily chopped
sea salt and milled black pepper
15 ml (1 Tbsp) balsamic vinegar
200 g fusilli tricolore (mixed pasta screws)
1 x 400 g can borlotti beans, drained and rinsed
30 g (about 500 ml/2 cups) rocket, torn
75 ml (5 Tbsp) grated Parmesan or pecorino cheese
45–60 ml (3–4 Tbsp) roasted pine nuts*

Heat the oil in a large frying pan, add the spring onions, garlic, red pepper and courgettes and stir-fry for a few minutes before adding the mushrooms. Toss until softening, then remove from the stove, season, and add the vinegar. Tip the just-cooked and drained (not rinsed) pasta into a bowl, add the beans, the stir-fry mixture with all its juices, and the rocket. Toss gently until combined, cool, then cover loosely and leave for an hour or so.** Just before serving, fork in the cheese and check the seasoning. Serve on a big platter, topped with the pine nuts. **Serves 6.**

*The pine nuts are not listed as a garnish as they are an integral part of the salad, but because they're so expensive you want to see them, and that is why they're on top. When roasting, do it properly – that is, let them get really nut-brown – it makes a huge difference to the flavour.

**This salad should be served at room temperature. If you have to make it in advance, it can be refrigerated (in a covered glass bowl) for up to a day, but it will lose out on the fine flavour.

VEGETARIAN
main courses

VEG AND CHICKPEA STEW
with olive bread

A favourite vegetarian dish of slow-simmered vegetables in a sauce spiked with cinnamon and topped with cheese –
so easy anyone can make it, and the bread is not complicated either. It is mixed in minutes, plopped into a cake tin,
smoothed out, left to rise, then baked. Serve fresh and warm – or reheat for about 10 minutes in a moderate oven.

VEG AND CHICKPEA STEW

60 ml (¼ cup) olive oil

1 large onion, halved and sliced into crescents

2 x 200 g aubergines (brinjals), cut into chunks and
dégorged

2 sticks celery, thinly sliced

2 cloves garlic, crushed

500 g ripe tomatoes (not canned), skinned and chopped

2 ml (½ tsp) ground cinnamon

1 fat stick cinnamon

10 ml (2 tsp) tomato paste

10 ml (2 tsp) honey

250 ml (1 cup) vegetable stock or water

1 x 410 g can chickpeas, rinsed and drained

a little sea salt to taste

lots of crumbled feta cheese for topping

Heat the oil in a large saucepan. Add the onion and,
when soft and golden, add the aubergines. Toss
around to coat the chunks with oil, then add the
celery, garlic, tomatoes, cinnamon, tomato paste,
honey and stock. Mix, then cover and simmer very
gently for 30 minutes, stirring now and then to mash
up the tomatoes. Add the chickpeas and a little extra
stock or water if you think it necessary, then continue
simmering for a further 15–20 minutes, until the
vegetables are softly mingled, and the sauce
thickened. Check the seasoning, remove the
cinnamon stick, sprinkle with feta and serve when
heated through – or serve as is, and pass the feta
separately. **Serves 4, and is easily doubled.**

OLIVE BREAD WITH PINE NUTS AND GARLIC

4 x 250 ml (4 cups) white bread flour

7 ml (1½ tsp) sea salt

15 ml (1 Tbsp) honey

15 ml (1 Tbsp) instant dry yeast

4 fat cloves garlic, crushed

a small handful of chopped curly- or flat-leaf parsley

2 pickling onions, coarsely grated

100 g calamata olives, rinsed, stoned and halved

30 ml (2 Tbsp) olive oil

45–60 ml (3–4 Tbsp) pine nuts

about 375 ml (1½ cups) very warm but not hot-hot water

pine nuts and 2 fresh sprigs of rosemary for topping

Mix all the ingredients, except the water and topping,
in a large bowl. Slowly mix in 250 ml (1 cup) of the
warm water. The batter will still be a little dry. Add
the rest of the water and, stirring briskly, mix to a
soft, sticky batter. You may need an extra 5–10 ml
(1–2 tsp) water to make it sloppy enough without
being wet. Have ready a round cake tin*, 22 x 7 cm,
first lightly oiled and then lined, base and sides,
with baking paper. Scoop the batter into the tin and
spread it out evenly with the back of a dampened
spoon. Press the rosemary and pine nuts lightly into
the top, cover with a cloth and leave for 1 hour until
risen almost to the top of the tin. (Instant yeast is
usually quick, but the batter is heavy due to the
olives, and therefore takes longer.) When puffed up,
bake on the middle shelf of the oven at 200 °C for
20 minutes, then reduce the heat to 180 °C and bake
for 20 minutes more – it should be nicely browned.
Leave for 10 minutes, run a spatula round the sides,
then turn out onto a rack, remove paper, and tap the
bottom – if it sounds hollow, the bread is done.

* If using a springform tin, put a tray underneath in
case of oil drips.

MUSHROOM RISOTTO
with tassies, spinach and pine nuts

It's moist and creamy with a pinkish tinge (the Tassies), a few threads of green (the spinach) and – the starring ingredient – chunks of portabellini mushrooms. If unavailable, substitute brown mushrooms.

900 ml (3⅗ cups) well-seasoned chicken stock

3 cloves garlic, crushed

30 ml (2 Tbsp) olive oil

15 ml (1 Tbsp) butter

1 medium onion, finely chopped

2 rashers lean, unsmoked back bacon (optional)

250 g portabellini mushrooms, wiped and quartered

300 ml (1⅕ cups) arborio rice

2 ml (½ tsp) freshly grated nutmeg

150 ml (⅗ cup) Tassenberg (or a dry red of choice)

2 large handfuls (about 60 g) baby spinach

sea salt and milled black pepper

45 ml (3 Tbsp) freshly grated Parmesan or pecorino cheese

30–45 ml (2–3 Tbsp) toasted pine nuts

Heat the stock with the garlic and keep the liquid warm on a stove plate set to low. Heat the oil and butter in a wide-based, heavy saucepan, and add the onion and bacon. (In Italy they would use pancetta; substitute bacon, or leave it out altogether.) When the onion turns golden and the bacon (if using) starts frying, add the mushrooms and toss for a few minutes. You'll find that they won't shrink like most mushrooms do, so just cook them briefly before tipping in the rice and the nutmeg. Use a wooden spoon to stir gently until coated, then slowly add the red wine. When absorbed, start adding the hot stock – do this in small cupfuls, waiting until each is absorbed before continuing. The whole process takes about 30 minutes. Tear the spinach roughly, add it, together with the seasoning, then remove from the stove – the spinach will wilt almost immediately. Mix in the Parmesan and pine nuts, and leave to stand, covered, for 2 minutes before serving in deep pasta bowls. Pass extra Parmesan for sprinkling, a bottle of superior olive oil for those who want it, and serve a plain green salad on the side. **Serves 4.**

GREEN RISOTTO
with butternut, pine nuts and asparagus

An unusual risotto, a novel colour, and a memorable taste experience. The asparagus is served separately –
use your fingers, and nibble as you go.

400 g butternut, peeled, cut into small dice
(prepared weight)
a good sprinkling of ground cinnamon
a trickle of runny honey
1.125 litres (4½ cups) vegetable stock
enough Swiss chard, cooked and well drained,
to provide 125 ml (½ cup) tightly packed
1 large onion, finely chopped
45 ml (3 Tbsp) each olive oil and butter
375 ml (1½ cups) arborio rice
2 ml (½ tsp) freshly grated nutmeg
45 ml (3 Tbsp) freshly grated Parmesan or
pecorino cheese
sea salt to taste
poached asparagus and toasted pine nuts for topping

Cook the butternut in the minimum of salted water –
use a wide frying pan, spread it out in a single layer,
sprinkle with cinnamon, drizzle with honey, and
simmer until just tender. Set aside. Blend the stock
and cooked Swiss chard in a blender (probably in
two batches) until smooth and about as green as
lucerne. Heat it. Soften the onion in the oil and butter
in a large, deep saucepan, add the rice and nutmeg,
toss to coat, then slowly add the hot stock, in small
doses, waiting until each dose is absorbed before
stirring in another. Don't hurry the process – be
prepared to stand there for about 30 minutes, by
which time the rice should be creamy. Carefully fold
in the butternut plus any juices left in its pan, then,
off the heat, fold in the cheese and salt. Cover with a
cloth and leave for a few minutes before ladling into
deep bowls or soup plates. Pass the asparagus and
pine nuts in separate bowls. Extra Parmesan makes a
good but optional addition. **Serves 6, with a salad.**

BAKED RICE AND VEG with omelette topping

In this dish the vegetables are first sautéed, then baked with the uncooked rice and herbs, resulting in maximum flavour with the minimum of fuss and a lovely aroma. The omelette, sliced into strips for the topping, finishes it off beautifully. Serve with a tossed green salad.

60 ml (¼ cup) oil

1 onion, chopped

2 leeks, white part only, sliced

2 cloves garlic, crushed

250 g brown mushrooms, wiped and sliced

4 young carrots, julienned

2 sticks celery, plus some leaves, chopped

375 ml (1½ cups) uncooked brown rice, rinsed

125 ml (½ cup) chopped fresh parsley

800 ml (3⅕ cups) hot vegetable or Marmite stock

sea salt and milled black pepper

30–45 ml (2–3 Tbsp) finely chopped fresh mixed herbs*

30 ml (2 Tbsp) soy sauce

125 ml (½ cup) toasted slivered almonds

a few pats of butter

Heat the oil in a large pan and lightly fry the onion, leeks and garlic. Add the mushrooms, carrots and celery and stir-fry for a few minutes until glistening, smelling good and starting to soften. Spoon into a 20 x 30 cm baking dish, add the rice, parsley, stock, seasoning and herbs, stir to mix well, then cover and bake at 160 °C for about 1 hour 10 minutes, or until the rice is cooked and the stock absorbed. Fork in the soy sauce, almonds and butter.

OMELETTE TOPPING

Make this a few minutes before the dish is done. Lightly mix 8–10 free-range eggs with a little water, salt and pepper. Cook half the mixture in an omelette pan (or lightly oiled frying pan) at a time. When just set, tilt the pan and roll the omelette over a few times, slide onto a plate and slice thinly. Arrange the slices on top of the rice dish as it comes out of the oven. **Serves 6.**

* Good mix: rosemary, thyme, marjoram and oregano.

CHICKPEA CURRY with mango and mint raita

A mild, spicy vegetarian dish; serve on fragrant rice with the raita on the side.

30 ml (2 Tbsp) oil
1 large onion, finely chopped
2–3 cloves garlic, crushed
1 yellow pepper, seeded, ribs removed, and sliced
20 ml (4 tsp) curry powder (or more)
5 ml (1 tsp) each ground cumin and coriander
2 ml (½ tsp) each ground cinnamon and turmeric
500 g really ripe tomatoes, skinned and chopped*
375 ml (1½ cups) vegetable stock
15 ml (1 Tbsp) tomato paste
2 bay leaves
a little sea salt
a trickle of runny honey
750 ml (3 cups) cooked chickpeas OR 2 x 400 g cans,
drained and rinsed
a handful of chopped fresh parsley
toasted cashew nuts, chopped, for topping (optional)

Heat the oil in a large saucepan, add the onion, garlic and yellow pepper and, when softening, add the spices. Stir briefly to release the flavours, adding, if necessary, a dash of water to prevent scorching. Stir in the remaining ingredients, except the cashews, bring to the boil, then cover and simmer very gently for about 35 minutes. Stir occasionally to mash up the tomatoes. Check seasoning, and if the sauce needs thickening, tilt the lid of the saucepan for the last few minutes. Remove the bay leaves, spoon into a heated serving dish and top with the cashews, if using. **Serves 4–6.**

* A 400 g can (plus the juice) could, at a pinch, be substituted, but then you will probably have to reduce the amount of stock by about 125 ml (½ cup).

MANGO AND MINT RAITA

For the raita, mix 250 ml (1 cup) thick Bulgarian yoghurt, a few chopped spring onions, a pinch of salt, about 125 ml (½ cup) diced, ripe mango and shredded fresh mint leaves (start with 12) in a small bowl, cover and refrigerate while the curry cooks. Just before serving, sprinkle with garam masala.

FRAGRANT ROASTED VEG
with minted bulgur and swirled yoghurt

This is a complete change from roasted Mediterranean vegetables with herbs, and the different colours, flavours and textures are stunning: bright, spiced vegetables, a pilaff with green peas, and a yoghurt dressing marbled with fresh herbs. It might all sound rather too much, but preparation is easy – the only time-consuming part is preparing the veg, but the pilaff and dressing can be quickly made while they are roasting, and it's worth it for the end result.

500 g butternut, peeled and diced (prepared weight)

300 g (about 12) patty pan squash, halved

130 g (about 14 spears) baby corn

125 g (about 5) baby carrots, julienned

250 g (about 8) peeled baby onions, halved root to tip

10 ml (2 tsp) cumin seeds

60 ml (¼ cup) olive oil

15 ml (1 Tbsp) butter

2 ml (½ tsp) ground cinnamon

5 ml (1 tsp) ground ginger

7 ml (1½ tsp) sea salt

15 ml (1 Tbsp) runny honey

Place all the prepared vegetables in your largest baking dish – never mind if they're a bit jumbled up, they might be too bulky to lie in a single layer. Then stand back and look – it's like a dishful of sunshine. Quickly dry-roast the cumin seeds in a small pan until they pop, then crush – use a rolling pin or a pestle. Heat the oil, butter, crushed cumin, cinnamon, ginger, salt and honey in a small saucepan until just melted together, then drizzle over the vegetables. Use your hands to toss everything together until shiny – if working ahead, you can cover and set the dish aside for an hour or two. Bake, covered, at 200 °C for 30 minutes, then toss the vegetables around a bit and bake, uncovered, for a further 30–45 minutes until cooked and tender. (If dinner is delayed, they won't mind being left to languish for a while in the switched-off oven.)

MINTED BULGUR PILAFF

10 ml (2 tsp) each olive oil and butter

6 spring onions, chopped

250 ml (1 cup) bulgur

750 ml (3 cups) hot water

5 ml (1 tsp) sea salt

250 ml (1 cup) cooked green peas

6–8 fresh mint leaves, chopped

Heat the oil and butter in a wide-based saucepan, add the spring onions, toss for a minute, then add the bulgur, water and salt. Stir to mix, then cover and simmer over very low heat for about 20 minutes until the water has been absorbed. Lightly mix in the peas and mint and, if liked, an extra knob of butter.

HERBED YOGHURT DRESSING

375 ml (1½ cups) thick, low-fat Bulgarian yoghurt

125 ml (½ cup) chopped fresh parsley

60 ml (¼ cup) fresh coriander leaves

10 ml (2 tsp) runny honey

2 ml (½ tsp) ground cumin

a pinch of sea salt

Place all the ingredients in a blender and pulse a few times until the herbs are fairly finely chopped and the mixture swirled with green.

Serve the roasted vegetables surrounded by the pilaff, with the dressing either drizzled over or served separately. If you'd like a garnish, roasted pine nuts are a lovely option, and you need only a smattering. **Serves 4 (with seconds) or 6 (with average appetites).**

simply splendid VEGETABLE CURRY

This one would feel right at home in the Karoo – simple country cooking, using pumpkin, sweet potatoes, spices and chutney – all adding up to a fragrant dish for winter.

45 ml (3 Tbsp) oil and a pat of butter

1 large onion, chopped

3 cloves garlic, chopped

15 ml (1 Tbsp) finely chopped, peeled root ginger

30 ml (2 Tbsp) curry powder

5 ml (1 tsp) each ground cumin and turmeric

300 g peeled, cubed pumpkin or butternut
(peeled weight)*

300 g peeled, cubed sweet potatoes (peeled weight)

1 x 410 g can whole tomatoes, chopped, plus juice

45 ml (3 Tbsp) chutney

250 ml (1 cup) vegetable stock

1 fat stick cinnamon

a handful of chopped fresh parsley

sea salt to taste

250–300 g small broccoli florets

fresh lemon juice

roasted cashew nuts and garam masala for topping

Heat the oil and butter in a very large, deep frying pan (28 x 7 cm) and sauté the onion, garlic and ginger. Add the spices and cook for a minute, then add the pumpkin and sweet potatoes, and toss to mix with the spices – add a dash of water if it seems dry. Add the remaining ingredients except the broccoli, lemon juice, cashews and garam masala. Stir to mix, then cover and simmer over very low heat for 30 minutes until the vegetables are nearly cooked. Gently stir in the broccoli and simmer, covered, until the vegetables are tender but holding their shape and the juices reduced and slightly thickened. Much depends on the size of the pan – you may have to add extra stock – up to 250 ml (1 cup). Add a dash of lemon juice to bring out the flavour, remove the cinnamon, spoon the curry into a heated serving dish and top with the nuts and garam masala. **Serves 6**.

* Use a pumpkin that has firm, bright orange flesh – if it is pale and watery, use butternut instead.

butter bean, mushroom and walnut **CURRY**

This easy, stove-top dish has quite a lively tang, and a surprising colour – pale caramel – which looks good on fragrant yellow rice. It's easy to double up, which might be a wise step, as second helpings are often called for.*

45 ml (3 Tbsp) oil
1 large onion, finely chopped
½–1 small fresh red chilli, seeded and shredded
15 ml (1 Tbsp) curry powder
2 ml (½ tsp) each ground cumin, cinnamon and turmeric
45 ml (3 Tbsp) flour
250 ml (1 cup) hot vegetable stock
250 ml (1 cup) milk (preferably low-fat)
a little sea salt and a pinch of sugar
15 ml (1 Tbsp) tomato paste
200 g brown mushrooms, wiped and coarsely chopped
1 red pepper, seeded, ribs removed, and diced
125 ml (½ cup) coarsely chopped walnuts
1 x 400 g can choice-grade butter beans, drained, rinsed
fresh lemon juice

* Double the sauce and use quick-cooking vegetables (julienned carrots, courgettes (baby marrows), baby corn). Borlottis can be substituted for the butter beans.

Heat the oil in a wide, heavy saucepan or large frying pan. Add the onion and chilli and fry very lightly, then add the spices and sizzle for a minute. Sprinkle in the flour, stirring to mix and adding a dash of water if dry, then slowly stir in the stock and milk. Allow to thicken over low heat, then add the seasoning and tomato paste. Cover and simmer – the sauce should just pop – for 10 minutes. Stir occasionally to prevent sticking. Sauté the mushrooms, red pepper and walnuts in 15 ml (1 Tbsp) each oil and butter until the mushrooms are just softening, then stir them into the sauce along with the beans, and simmer until heated through, OR omit this step and simply add these ingredients to the sauce and simmer until the mushrooms are cooked. Check the seasoning, and add a little extra stock if necessary – the mixture should be really moist. Add a dash of lemon juice to sharpen the flavour. Serve with chutney and a green salad.
Serves 4–5.

QUICK CHILLI BEANS
with corn and avocado

This is one of those speedy suppers that doesn't fall down on flavour despite the haste.
Best served on couscous, but brown rice is also good.

½–2 red chillies, chopped*

1 small green pepper, seeded, ribs removed, and diced

1 x 400 g can chopped tomatoes in juice**

1–2 cloves garlic, crushed

30 ml (2 Tbsp) soft brown sugar

1 small onion, finely chopped

125 ml (½ cup) water

15 ml (1 Tbsp) red wine vinegar

a large pinch of sea salt

1 x 400 g can choice-grade butter beans, drained
  and rinsed

250 ml (1 cup) cooked corn kernels (use fresh or frozen)

1 avocado, thinly sliced or cubed

milled black pepper to taste

To make the sauce you'll need a large, deep frying pan as the beans get added to it and butter beans are voluptuously plump. Combine the chillies, green pepper, tomatoes, garlic, sugar, onion, water, vinegar and salt in the pan. Stir to mix, bring to the boil, immediately reduce the heat, cover and simmer very gently for about 30 minutes until slightly thickened. Add the beans and the corn and simmer for 5–10 minutes, until very hot. Check seasoning, turn into a heated serving dish, top prettily with the avo (which is not a garnish, it is important to the dish), grind over the pepper and serve. I also like a splosh of yoghurt on the side – it cools the chilli and the colour contrast is pleasing. **Serves 4, easily doubled.**

* Chillies differ enormously with regard to heat – it depends on the colour, the size, and whether you add the seeds or not. The amount and type of chilli used here depends on the choice of the cook, so it's a good idea to swot them up.

** These differ in density from cans of whole peeled tomatoes – they are interchangeable, but you might have to adjust the quantity of liquid in the recipe.

ROASTED VEGETABLES
in a creamy tomato sauce

This one is for hungry diners: chunky veg in a rosy sauce laced with herbs, bolstered with borlottis, and served on fettucine. Put out grated Parmesan, a crusty loaf and olive oil, and they'll be happy for hours.

400 g aubergines (brinjals), diced, dégorged, rinsed, dried

350 g courgettes (baby marrows), pared and chunked (prepared weight)

2 red peppers, seeded, ribs removed, sliced into strips

1 large onion, cut into 10 wedges

4 plump cloves garlic, crushed

5 ml (1 tsp) dried oregano

a little sea salt

60 ml (¼ cup) olive oil

about 400 g fettucine

SAUCE

2 x 410 g cans tomatoes (try for whole Italian), chopped, plus juice

2 medium carrots, diced

1 medium onion, chopped

1 large stick celery, plus leaves, chopped

15 ml (1 Tbsp) tomato paste

125 ml (½ cup) red wine

30 ml (2 Tbsp) olive oil

10 ml (2 tsp) sugar and a little sea salt

125 ml (½ cup) fresh basil leaves, or basil and parsley mixed

1 x 410 g can borlotti beans, drained and rinsed (you can substitute cannellini beans or chickpeas)

Place all the vegetables in a large baking dish, sprinkle with oregano and salt, toss with the oil and roast, uncovered, at 220 °C for 40 minutes (toss once) until soft, sizzling and starting to brown. For the sauce, place all the ingredients, except the basil and beans, in a large saucepan. Bring to the boil, cover and simmer over very low heat for 45 minutes, until cooked and intensely red and juicy. Cool before puréeing in a blender, in batches, until smooth. Return to the saucepan, add the roasted vegetables, basil and beans. When piping hot, serve with the just-cooked pasta. If the sauce is too thick, add a little stock, but keep it voluptuous. **Serves 6–8.**

DESSERTS

lemon or strawberry **MERINGUE**

If you put the meringue at the bottom and the filling on top, you avoid the pitfall of a weepy meringue pie. This is a fairly tart tart, not overly sweet and it's refreshingly lemony, topped with candied lemon peel (easy to make, page 155, leaving out the ginger). If you prefer a fruity, creamy filling, try the Strawberry Meringue, which could also fill a pavlova.

MERINGUE

4 XL free-range egg whites (at room temperature)
0.5 ml (⅛ tsp) salt
0.5 ml (⅛ tsp) cream of tartar
250 ml (1 cup) castor sugar

For the meringue shell, whisk the egg whites until foamy. Add the salt and cream of tartar and whisk until stiff. Gradually add the castor sugar, whisking constantly until the mixture becomes very thick and glossy. Shape the meringue into a 22 cm circle on a large baking tray lined with two sheets of baking paper – do not grease anything, and use a regular-type tray, not a coated one. (To secure the paper, use a dollop of meringue below each corner.) Using the back of a spoon, gently flatten the centre and push the sides outwards to form a rim. Bake at 150 °C for 15 minutes, then at 120 °C for 1 hour – don't open the oven door at any stage. Switch off the oven and leave the shell until absolutely cold – even overnight. Just before you are ready to fill it, gently remove the baking paper and place the shell on a large platter. Work carefully; the meringue is fragile.

LEMON FILLING

4 XL free-range egg yolks (saved from the meringue)
60 ml (¼ cup) fresh lemon juice
5 ml (1 tsp) finely grated lemon rind
125 ml (½ cup) castor sugar
250 ml (1 cup) milk
40 ml (8 tsp) cornflour
250 ml (1 cup) cream
5 ml (1 tsp) vanilla essence
candied lemon peel for topping (page 155)

Whisk together the egg yolks, lemon juice and rind, castor sugar, milk and cornflour. Pour into a heavy-based saucepan and stir over very low heat until cooked – using a balloon whisk should avoid any troublesome lumps, as the mixture becomes very thick, rather like porridge. When cooked, scrape into a mixing bowl, and leave to cool, stirring occasionally. Whip the cream with the vanilla until stiff, give the custard a quick last whisk to make sure it's absolutely smooth, then add to the cream in small dollops, gently folding in each addition until everything is smoothly combined. Turn into the meringue shell (do this with care, a heavy plop will crack the shell), and spread evenly. Sprinkle with the candied peel and refrigerate until the filling firms up – 3–4 hours. Longer than that, and the meringue will become soft. **Serves 10.**

STRAWBERRY FILLING

Other fruits such as mangoes and bananas could, of course, be added, but there's something very summery and enticing about a pure strawberry meringue.

250 g ripe, red strawberries
10 ml (2 tsp) castor sugar
5 ml (1 tsp) balsamic vinegar
250 ml (1 cup) cream
30 ml (2 Tbsp) icing sugar
25 ml (5 tsp) Amaretto liqueur
a few drops of vanilla essence

Rinse and hull the strawberries and slice enough of them into fairly small pieces to fill a 250 ml (1 cup) measure. Reserve the remaining berries for decoration. Place the sliced berries in a single layer on a large plate and sprinkle over the castor sugar and vinegar, leave for about 30 minutes, then pour off the juices that will have drawn. Pat dry with paper towel. Whip the cream with the icing sugar, liqueur and vanilla, fold in the berries and spoon into the meringue shell. Decorate with the remaining berries and serve, or refrigerate briefly. **Serves 8–10.**

spicy **POACHED NECTARINES**

This is a fine example of perfect fruit needing little embellishment: freestone nectarines, halved, poached with spices, and served with pouring cream. A bonus is that it needs to be made well in advance, and you could add a tot of orange liqueur to the cream if you wish.

4–6 (600–700 g) firm, almost-ripe, freestone nectarines
8–12 whole cloves
500 ml (2 cups) water
125 ml (½ cup) light brown sugar
2 sticks cinnamon
2 x 5 cm strips orange peel

Place the nectarines in a large bowl, pour boiling water over to cover, and leave to stand for about 1 minute. Drain in a colander and, as soon as the nectarines are cool enough to handle, slip off the skins, separate into two halves and discard the pips. Push a clove into the rounded side of each half. Bring the water, sugar, cinnamon sticks and orange peel to the boil in a large frying pan, stirring until the sugar has dissolved, then slide the halved nectarines into the syrup to lie in a single layer. Reduce the heat immediately, then cover and poach gently for about 15 minutes. Test with a thin skewer, and if it slips in easily, they're done – be sure not to over-poach so that they become flaccid. Using a slotted spoon, remove the nectarines to a fairly large, fairly shallow, heat-resistant serving bowl, in a single layer (don't remove the cloves). Now boil the syrup rapidly until reduced by about half, bubbly, and the palest caramel in colour. Strain the syrup over the nectarines, leave to cool, and refrigerate for 24 hours. Serve two halves per diner, pouring over some of the syrup, and passing a jug of cream.
Serves 4–6.

ALMOND-ROASTED PEACHES with schnapps

When peaches are in season it's tempting to serve them pure and fresh. There's something about sitting on a patio with peach juice dribbling down your chin that simply melts you with the joy of summer and sea and sun – but when a formal occasion demands that you fiddle with them a little in order to turn them into more of a dessert, then this is the answer. A quick dip and sprinkle, followed by a short bake – and out they come, soft and juicy and ready for serving either with thick cream or crème Chantilly. I must admit that, in this recipe, the schnapps is incidental – hardly even a suggestion – but it does add a little sweetness, and I included it in the title because it sounds so tempting.

large, ripe but unbruised freestone dessert peaches (about 150 g each)
melted butter
toasted almond flakes, crushed*
ground cinnamon
castor sugar
peach schnapps (optional)

Wash the peaches well, run a knife round the centre seams and halve. Discard the pips. Removing the skin is optional – I prefer to do this, especially if they are not organic peaches – but in any case, if they are ripe, it's a doddle to slip off the skin. Melt some butter and pour onto a large plate. Press each peach half, cut side down, into the butter, making sure to moisten well, then press into the almonds – be generous here. Arrange the peaches, cut sides up, in a lightly buttered baking dish to fit closely together. Sprinkle each with cinnamon – use your fingers rather than a spoon, to avoid clumps of the spice, then finish with a sprinkling of castor sugar. (One doesn't need much, the peaches are sweet anyway.) Bake at 200 °C for about 20 minutes until succulent and, if using the schnapps, spoon 5 ml (1 tsp) into each hollow as you take the peaches out of the oven.

* Don't use ready-ground almonds. Buy flakes, roast them lightly, and crush fairly finely – a rolling pin used on a breadboard does the job perfectly.

ORANGES VAN DER HUM
with candied orange peel

I have used different ways of serving sliced orange desserts – macerated with spices, in a whisky syrup, or in melting sugar with a rich sabayon. All good – but this recipe has a more ethnic flavour and is easy and refreshing.

4 large or 6 medium, sweet, navel oranges (about 800 g)
125 ml (½ cup) sugar
125 ml (½ cup) fresh orange juice
45 ml (3 Tbsp) Van der Hum liqueur

Peel the oranges, remove all the white pith, and slice across into thin rings. Arrange in a flattish, heatproof dish – a 23–26 cm pie dish is ideal. Some slices will overlap, just squish them in gently until they're all lying flat. Spread the sugar out into a heavy, medium frying pan and allow to caramelise over low heat. You can stir occasionally just to spread it out, but mainly you should just shake the pan – it takes a while over low heat. Remove from the stove when it's a really deep toffee colour (no more, or it will scorch) and slowly and very carefully stir in the orange juice. The mixture will seize immediately, and make all sorts of weird tentacle-like shapes, but keep stirring and, if necessary put back on a low heat and stir until all the lumps have melted. Pour the syrup over the oranges, and then sprinkle the liqueur over evenly. Cool, cover and refrigerate for 2 days. Serve as is, or sprinkle with candied orange peel. **Serves 5–6 with ice cream.**

CANDIED ORANGE PEEL

Julienne the peel of 2 large oranges (having removed all the white pith). In a small saucepan, melt 60 ml (4 Tbsp) sugar in 60 ml (¼ cup) water. Add the orange strips and cook over high heat until caramelized, then just cover with cold water and a lid and simmer slowly until soft. Remove from heat and leave to cool; the juices will slowly be absorbed. Sprinkle over the oranges before serving.

CREAMY, RUMMY FRUIT SALAD
with crunchy pecans

I think seriously rich desserts are a fabulous treat in a restaurant because eating out is (usually) an occasional treat, but I don't like making a habit of serving them at home. I once saw a guest hide her incredibly rich but utterly superb (I didn't make it) chocolate terrine behind the dining-room curtain at the back of her chair, because she was full after two spoonfuls, but did not want to offend her hostess. It's true. And that's one of the reasons why I like serving a fruit salad – tart it up, give it a fancy name, and everyone can finish it. Tropical fruits are the best.

4 mangoes (about 1.1 kg), peeled and cubed

4 bananas, sliced and tossed in lemon juice

400 g peeled and cubed papino (prepared weight)

12–16 fresh or canned litchis, pitted and slivered

150 ml (⅗ cup) thick, low-fat Bulgarian yoghurt

150 ml (⅗ cup) crème fraîche

30 ml (2 Tbsp) pale, runny honey (fynbos is a good choice)

30 ml (2 Tbsp) dark rum

TOPPING

30 ml (2 Tbsp) soft brown sugar

15 ml (1 Tbsp) butter

30 ml (2 Tbsp) water

about 125 ml (½ cup) pecan nut halves or quarters

Mix all the fruit gently in a beautiful glass bowl – wide, rather than deep. Mix the remaining ingredients; don't whisk, just stir until smoothly combined, then pour over the fruit, cover and refrigerate for 3–4 hours.

For the topping, melt the sugar and butter in the water in a small pan over low heat. Add the pecans and toss until crunchy. Drain on a paper towel, set aside, and sprinkle over the fruit salad just before serving. **Serves 8–10.**

strawberry-amaretto **SYLLABUB**

There was a time when, in order to make syllabub, you had to milk a cow into a bowl. There's a lot more to the story, but suffice it to say that dozens of new versions of this dessert have evolved over the years, and you no longer need a cow in order to make it. But the basics are almost always a tipple of alcohol and a lot of cream, and this version, incorporating berries and liqueur, is superb. Presentation is important, but apart from that it's one of the easiest, most luscious, do-ahead desserts imaginable.

400–450 g sweet, ripe strawberries
60 ml (¼ cup) castor sugar
60 ml (¼ cup) Amaretto liqueur
a squeeze, about 5 ml (1 tsp), fresh lemon juice
a little milled black pepper (optional)
250 ml (1 cup) thick cream
15 ml (1 Tbsp) icing sugar
toasted almond flakes for topping

Rinse, hull and dry the strawberries, then slice them thinly. Spread out in a large, shallow bowl, sprinkle with the castor sugar, liqueur and lemon juice, and cover and macerate for about 1 hour. By this time lovely juices will have been drawn. Carefully pour them off – you should have almost 125 ml (½ cup) – and set aside. Spoon the strawberries into six red wine glasses – use glasses (or goblets for that matter) that are roundish rather than longish. If using the pepper, give a quick twist over each nest of berries – just a little. Whip the cream lightly, adding the icing sugar as you go. Slowly drizzle in the reserved juices and whip until thickish – firmer than floppy, but not stiff. Spoon over the berries; there's heaps of cream so you'll be able to pile it high. (In fact, there's enough for another helping of berries.) Sprinkle generously with almond flakes. Place the glasses on a flat tray so that they don't fall over, and transfer to the coldest part of the fridge for the rest of the day (6–8 hours). By serving time, the cream should have just started to melt and trickle down to the berries. Eat with small spoons. **Serves 6.**

strawberry and mint **SOFT-SERVES**

This is quickly whizzed in a blender to a thick, pink creaminess, like a soft-serve, but instead of coming in a cone, the mixture is spooned into parfait or wine glasses or goblets, and refrigerated until just firm enough to be scooped up with small spoons. The minimum quantity of gelatine is used to achieve the softly set texture, while the elusive fragrance of fresh mint (just a snitch is necessary) comes through now and then to offset the richness. This dessert is a real quick 'n easy one, and offers a slightly new take on the popular combo of strawberries and cream.

500 g ripe, bright red strawberries
10 ml (2 tsp) gelatine
30 ml (2 Tbsp) water
250 ml (1 cup) cream
180 ml (¾ cup) sifted icing sugar
5 ml (1 tsp) vanilla essence
1 x 250 g tub smooth, low-fat cottage cheese
10 ml (2 tsp) finely shredded fresh mint leaves

Rinse and hull the berries, pat absolutely dry, then chop into small pieces. For a velvety soft-serve, whizz all the berries in a blender until smooth; for a slightly chunkier texture, reserve one-quarter of the chopped berries, and fold these in later, along with the mint.

Sprinkle the gelatine onto the water in a small container, then dissolve over simmering water – do not overheat. Add to the strawberry purée and pulse briefly to mix. Whip the cream with the icing sugar and vanilla essence until stiff, then gently stir in the cottage cheese until it's all nice and smooth. Add the purée and the mint, then fold in the reserved chopped berries, if using this option. Keep folding over gently until combined but not uniformly pink – a slightly marbled effect is attractive. Pour, or spoon, into six to eight glasses or goblets and place in the coldest part of the refrigerator to firm up – a few hours, or even overnight, loosely covered. Decoration is optional – although mint leaves have become boring and dated, a tiny sprig would actually be appropriate, otherwise a small strawberry, if you have any left, otherwise leave plain. **Serves 6–8.**

apple and mango
CRUMBLE

There's hardly a fruit that hasn't been turned into a crumble, for the simple reason that when it comes to homespun, comforting desserts, crumbles are probably top of the list. The following is another variation on the theme, with mango and coconut introducing a tropical touch, and cashews adding crunch.

1 x 765 g can unsweetened pie apple slices

1 x 410 g can mango slices, drained and syrup reserved

30 ml (2 Tbsp) golden syrup

30 ml (2 Tbsp) sugar

CRUMBLE*

375 ml (1½ cups) cake flour

5 ml (1 tsp) baking powder

a small pinch of sea salt

7 ml (1½ tsp) ground cinnamon

90 ml (6 Tbsp) castor sugar (or vanilla sugar if available)

90 ml (6 Tbsp) desiccated coconut

100 g butter, cubed

cashew nuts, halved or roughly chopped

If the apples are in large slices, chop into chunks. Chop the mango slices too. Place in a buttered 23 x 5 cm pie dish, pour over 125 ml (½ cup) of the reserved mango syrup, and mix in the golden syrup and sugar.

To make the crumble, place the flour, baking powder, salt and cinnamon in a processor fitted with the metal blade and pulse to mix, then add the castor sugar and coconut, pulse again, then add the butter and pulse until the mixture is finely crumbed. Sprinkle this over the fruit – it will be thickly covered – and finish with a scatter of cashews. Bake at 180 °C for 45 minutes until the crumble is toast-coloured and the syrup is bubbling through. Serve warm, rather than hot, with thick cream. **Serves 6–8.**

* If you'd prefer a more wholesome topping, mix 250 ml (1 cup) unsweetened muesli with 125 ml (½ cup) self-raising flour, 30 g chopped pecan nuts, 5 ml (1 tsp) ground cinnamon, 90 ml (6 Tbsp) light brown sugar and 125 ml (½ cup) oil.

baked
APPLE PUFF

... or Ouma's Winter Fruit Cobbler. A hearty, homespun pudding, large and sweet and easy to make.
Serve warm, rather than hot, with whipped cream or home-made custard.

1 x 765 g can unsweetened pie apple slices*
2 large bananas OR 2 large fresh pears OR 1 of each
125 ml (½ cup) golden syrup
100 ml (⅖ cup) hot water
60 ml (4 Tbsp) seedless raisins
250 ml (1 cup) self-raising flour
7 ml (1½ tsp) ground cinnamon
2 ml (½ tsp) freshly grated nutmeg
90 ml (6 Tbsp) light brown sugar
90 ml (6 Tbsp) desiccated coconut
250 ml (1 cup) oil
2 XL free-range eggs
a pinch of salt

Chop the apples into smaller pieces. Dice the bananas, or peel, core and dice the pears. Mix the apples and chosen fruit, and spoon into a lightly buttered 25–26 cm pie dish, at least 6 cm deep (or the syrup will bubble over). Melt the golden syrup in the water and pour over the fruit. Sprinkle in the raisins. Whisk the remaining ingredients together to make a thick batter, then simply drop in spoonfuls over the fruit – the batter will spread during baking. Bake at 180 °C for 35–40 minutes until the topping is lightly browned and firm. Remove from the oven carefully because of the bubbling syrup. Allow to cool down a little before serving. **Serves 8**.

* Use choice-grade pie apples, firmly packed, with no juice to speak of.

ORANGE BAVAROIS with hot chocolate sauce

Everything here can be done in advance, making this an ideal dessert when entertaining.

15 ml (1 Tbsp) gelatine
125 ml (½ cup) fresh orange juice
375 ml (1½ cups) milk
finely grated rind of 1 medium orange
2 XL free-range eggs, separated
60 ml (4 Tbsp) castor sugar
a small pinch of salt
a few drops of vanilla essence
125 ml (½ cup) cream, softly whipped

SAUCE

100 g plain milk chocolate, broken up
30 ml (2 Tbsp) pouring cream
30 ml (2 Tbsp) milk
20–30 ml (4–6 tsp) Van der Hum liqueur (optional)

Sprinkle the gelatine onto the orange juice and leave to sponge. Scald the milk with the orange rind – do this over low heat, in order to release the flavour. Whisk the egg yolks with the castor sugar until pale and thick. Using a fine sieve, slowly strain the hot milk onto the egg mixture, stir to mix, add a pinch of salt, then return to the saucepan and cook over very low heat, stirring, until the mixture coats the back of a wooden spoon. It has to thicken, but dare not boil. Remove from the stove, stir in the sponged gelatine and vanilla, give a quick whisk to make sure that all the gelatine has dissolved, then cool in a mixing bowl. Hurry this up by standing the mixing bowl in a bowl of cold water. Once cooled, it may be chilled briefly until just thickening, but not yet setting. Fold in the cream, and then the stiffly whisked egg whites – use a metal spoon and stir a spoonful through the mixture first, then fold in the remainder. Pour into eight rinsed ramekins (6 cm diameter, 5 cm deep) and refrigerate until set. Overnight, if you wish. Unmould the ramekins onto serving plates.

To make the sauce, melt the chocolate with the pouring cream and milk in a double boiler or saucepan over low heat. Stir occasionally until smooth – do not let it boil or bubble. Set aside. Add the liqueur and reheat gently just before serving. Drizzle a little of the hot sauce over, allowing it to run down the sides. **Serves 8.**

apple and pear **DESSERT CAKE**

This is a sweetly nostalgic pud, closely related to Eve's Pudding – the traditional, homely, sponge-topped apple dessert – but presented here with a few twists: pears with the apples, cinnamon and almonds in the topping. Serve warm with thick cream, crème fraîche or vanilla ice cream, or at room temperature, sliced into wedges.

500 g ripe Golden Delicious apples, peeled and chopped*
500 g ripe Packham's pears, peeled and chopped*
100 ml (⅖ cup) light brown sugar
seeds from 1 vanilla pod, or a few drops of vanilla essence
30 ml (2 Tbsp) water
125 g soft butter
100 ml (⅖ cup) castor sugar
2 large free-range eggs
250 ml (1 cup) self-raising flour
a pinch of sea salt
7 ml (1½ tsp) ground cinnamon
60 ml (4 Tbsp) ground almonds
30 ml (2 Tbsp) hot water

Stew the apples and pears with the brown sugar, vanilla and the 30 ml (2 Tbsp) water until soft. Keep the heat low so that the fruit will release its juices – about 12 minutes should do if the fruit is sweet and ripe. Spoon into a lightly buttered pie dish, 23 cm in diameter and about 5 cm deep. Cream the butter and castor sugar until pale and fluffy, then whisk in the eggs, one at a time, adding a pinch of flour with each egg. Sift in the flour, salt and cinnamon, and fold into the butter mixture along with the almonds. The batter will be thick and should now be lightened by folding in the hot water. Don't try to spread the batter over the fruit, just drop it all over, in big dollops – it will spread during baking. Bake at 180 °C for 35–40 minutes until golden brown and puffed up, with just a hole or a crack here and there with a bit of fruit peeking through. Serve warm, rather than hot.
Serves 6–8.

* Try to use these varieties, as they provide the correct texture and sweetness.

chocolate MOUSSE TRIFLE

This is neither a mousse nor a trifle, but there are elements of both in this dreamy combination of chocolate and cream set on a base of sliced swiss roll moistened with coffee and liqueur. It makes a special-occasion, party-sized dessert, to serve in wedges with ribbons of a fruity coulis as the perfect foil. Fresh strawberries whizzed with a touch of sugar are super, while lightly poached pears blended to a smooth purée are just as good with the chocolate-coffee flavours. May also be served in plump goblets. Drizzle a little coulis around the inside rims before serving.

1 jam-filled chocolate swiss roll (about 450 g)
125 ml (½ cup) warm, medium-strength black coffee
20 ml (4 tsp) quality coffee liqueur, e.g. Kahlúa
200 g dark chocolate
3 XL free-range egg whites
45 ml (3 Tbsp) castor sugar
250 ml (1 cup) cream
30 ml (2 Tbsp) icing sugar
a few drops of vanilla essence
chocolate scrolls to decorate (optional)

Cut the swiss roll into 1.5 cm thick slices and squish them in to fit tightly into a 25 cm diameter pie dish. Mix the coffee and liqueur and drizzle over evenly. Smear a small heatproof bowl with butter, add the broken-up chocolate and place over simmering water. Don't try to melt the chocolate; the blocks should just soften completely. Cool slightly. Meanwhile, whisk the egg whites until stiff, slowly add the castor sugar and whisk to a stiff meringue. Slowly add the soft chocolate in small dollops, whisking all the time. By the time it has all been incorporated, the meringue will have deflated somewhat – this is correct. Without washing the beaters, whisk the cream, icing sugar and vanilla essence until stiff. Gently fold into the chocolate-meringue, and pour over the swiss roll base. Use a spatula to spread evenly, then immediately place in the coldest part of the refrigerator and leave to firm up, loosely covered, for 24 hours before serving. Sprinkle with chocolate scrolls, if using, slice into thin wedges and use a spatula to transfer to serving plates. Drizzle coulis alongside, and serve immediately. **Serves 10–12.**

green fig and ginger **CHEESECAKE**

Fig and ginger preserves combine superbly, and here they add amazing flavour to a plump, fluffy cheesecake.

CRUST

125 ml (½ cup) each ginger and plain biscuit crumbs

75 ml (5 Tbsp) melted butter

FILLING

25 ml (5 tsp) gelatine

75 ml (5 Tbsp) cold water

a knob or two of ginger preserve, rinsed and patted dry

1 x 370 g jar green fig preserve, rinsed and patted dry

2 XL free-range egg whites

200 ml (⅘ cup) castor sugar

1 x 250 g tub cream cheese

1 x 250 g tub smooth, low-fat cottage cheese

250 ml (1 cup) cream

7 ml (1½ tsp) vanilla essence

sliced figs and ground cinnamon for topping

Mix the biscuit crumbs and butter, press onto the greased base of a deep 22–23 cm pie dish, and chill.

To make the filling, sponge the gelatine in the cold water, then dissolve over simmering water. Leave to cool. Finely chop enough ginger and figs to give you 30 ml (2 Tbsp) of each, and set aside. Whisk the egg whites until stiffening, then gradually whisk in half the castor sugar to make a glossy meringue. Whisk the remaining castor sugar with both tubs of cheese, the cream and the vanilla essence until smooth. Slowly, while whisking, add the cooled gelatine, then fold in the meringue. Pour half this mixture onto the chilled crust. Sprinkle over the chopped ginger and fig preserve, then cover with the remaining creamy mixture, spreading evenly. (Work quickly as it firms up fast.) Chill until set. Slice three or four of the remaining figs into thin rounds, arrange in a circle round the edge of the cheesecake and sprinkle the centre with cinnamon – either do this just before serving, or decorate and chill again until required, although the colour will fade a bit and the crust will soften, but this won't affect the flavour. Slice into wedges and remove with a spatula. **Serves 10.**

unsinkable baked **LEMON CHEESECAKE**

A favourite cheesecake, soft and creamy, that does not make waves in the baking, then collapse in the centre. The flat
top makes a perfect base for a spread of whipped cream and a sprinkling of lightly candied lemon peel and ginger.
For a lighter option, the cream can be omitted – simply sprinkle the cheesecake with ground cinnamon before baking.

CRUST
250 ml (1 cup) biscuit crumbs
60 ml (¼ cup) melted butter

FILLING
2 large free-range eggs
125 ml (½ cup) castor sugar
2 ml (½ tsp) vanilla essence
7 ml (1½ tsp) very finely grated lemon rind
30 ml (2 Tbsp) cornflour
2 x 250 g tubs smooth, low-fat cottage cheese,
drained of any liquid
150 ml (⅗ cup) thick cream

Mix the ingredients for the crust and press firmly onto the greased base (not the sides) of a 20 cm pie dish – use the back of a spoon to spread evenly. Bake at 160 °C for 10 minutes. Cool. To make the filling, whisk the eggs and sugar until pale and light, then add the vanilla, lemon rind, cornflour, cheese and cream. Whisk well until everything's combined, then pour onto the crust. Bake on the middle shelf of the oven at 180 °C for 20 minutes, then switch off the heat but don't open the door – just leave it there for 15 minutes more before removing it to cool – it will still be a bit wobbly. Once cooled, refrigerate until firm enough to slice. **Makes 8 wedges.**

CANDIED LEMON PEEL AND GINGER
Place in a small saucepan: 125 ml (½ cup) water; thinly julienned peel (or zest) of 1 medium lemon; 10 ml (2 tsp) peeled and very thinly sliced fresh root ginger (1 small knob). Simmer, covered, for 10 minutes or until softened, then add 15 ml (1 Tbsp) light brown sugar. Increase the heat and boil, uncovered, until lightly caramelized, shaking the pan regularly. Remove from the stove when just starting to catch; carefully add 30 ml (2 Tbsp) water and leave to cool and soften before sprinkling over the cheesecake.

chocolate frangelico **SEMIFREDDO**

Semifreddos are very rich, soft, frozen desserts often made with double cream, eggs and sugar, with a flavouring of choice. This version is not strictly traditional, but it's hard to beat for sheer delicious decadence. The mixture is set in a loaf-shaped container, frozen overnight, turned out and sliced for serving. It will start to melt almost immediately, which is what it should do, therefore have serving plates ready and waiting. If you want to set the slices on a pool of sorts, choose something bland like a fresh pear coulis – even custard would detract from the intense chocolate flavour. If not using a coulis, go for one or two sweet, scarlet strawberries – plain, or choc-dipped. They look fabulous placed alongside each slice.

40–50 g hazelnuts
200 ml (⅘ cup) light brown sugar
125 ml (½ cup) water
175 ml (scant ¾ cup) cocoa powder
3 large free-range eggs, separated
2 ml (½ tsp) vanilla essence
45 ml (3 Tbsp) Frangelico liqueur
250 ml (1 cup) cream, softly whipped
a small pinch of salt

Roast or grill the nuts until browned. Wrap them in a kitchen towel and rub vigorously to remove the loose skins, then chop the nuts coarsely. Place the sugar, water and cocoa powder in a small saucepan and melt over low heat, stirring (do not boil). Set aside to cool for about 10 minutes. Whisk the egg yolks, vanilla essence and liqueur very well until foamy. Gradually add the chocolate (cocoa) mixture, whisking well between additions. Fold in the cream and the nuts. Stiffly whisk two of the egg whites (you don't need the third) with the salt. Stir a dollop through the chocolate mixture, then gently fold in the remainder. Line a 1-litre freezerproof, loaf-shaped container with clingfilm (use enough for an overlap), pour in the 'freddo' and freeze at once. After a few hours it should be firm enough to cover the top with the overlapping clingwrap. Freeze for 24 hours. Unmould onto a large, flat plate, slice and serve.
Makes 10–12 slices.

amarula **PANNA COTTA**

Panna cottas are delicate 'cooked cream' desserts, usually made with sweetened double cream flavoured with vanilla and softly set with a flurry of gelatine. Once chilled and unmoulded, they look just like wobbly little blancmanges, but they're much richer and, because of this, a trend – outside of Italy – is to scale down the fat with the addition of milk, which of course requires extra gelatine, which could result in a rubbery wobble, which is all wrong. An attractive solution is to set the panna cottas in small coffee cups. Then, instead of unmoulding them, you simply place the cups on their saucers, with small spoons alongside. In this way it is still possible to use a proportion of milk without extra gelatine. This is an unusual presentation, but these little Amarula creams provide a seriously delicious ending to a fine dinner when something sweet – but small – would be just right.

7 ml (1½ tsp) gelatine
90 ml (6 Tbsp) Amarula liqueur
500 ml (2 cups) double cream
1 vanilla pod, split open lengthwise
250 ml (1 cup) milk
30 ml (2 Tbsp) castor sugar
cocoa powder for dusting

Sprinkle the gelatine over the liqueur in a small container and leave to sponge. Mix the cream, vanilla pod, milk and castor sugar in a heavy saucepan and bring to just below boiling point over very low heat, stirring occasionally. Remove the saucepan from the heat and stir in the sponged gelatine, making sure that it is all dissolved. Leave to cool, stirring now and then, then strain the cream into six coffee cups. Refrigerate for a few hours until softly set. Just before serving, sift a whisper of cocoa powder over the top of each – this is simply to add a little colour to the pale cream – then serve as suggested, on the day of making. **Serves 6**.

chocolate **FUDGE CUPS**

*I think the highest praise anyone can receive after hosting a dinner party is when one of the guests requests a recipe –
and this one always leaves the house, especially now that those 70% cocoa slabs are available. Not only is it a super
recipe, but it's a life-saver for reluctant dessert makers because, being so rich, it's absolutely acceptable to set it in small,
after-dinner coffee cups. Desserts stretch amazingly when all they have to do is fill a small cup (Amarula Panna Cotta,
previous page, is another fine example). So buy some stunning little cups and your dessert problems could be solved.*

1 x 100 g slab 70% Belgian Intense chocolate, broken up
(Swiss chocolate is second-best here)
1 x 100 g plain dark chocolate (e.g. Albany), broken up
10 ml (2 tsp) cocoa powder
500 ml (2 cups) whipping cream
5 ml (1 tsp) vanilla essence
30 ml (2 Tbsp) icing sugar
chocolate shavings for sprinkling – preferably white for
a colour contrast

Smear a small saucepan with a little butter (this
makes it easier to scrape out). Add the chocolate,
cocoa and 100 ml (⅖ cup) of the cream. Melt over
very low heat, stirring just a few times to get it going.
Remove from the heat as soon as the mixture is
smooth, and set aside until cool. Whip the remaining
cream with the vanilla and icing sugar until thick but
not stiff, then slowly whisk in the cooled chocolate
mixture in dollops – make about five additions
altogether, and stop as soon as everything is
smoothly combined and uniformly chocolate in
colour, being careful not to beat the life out of it.
Spoon into eight to ten little cups, sprinkle with
chocolate shavings and place (on their saucers so
that they don't fall over) in the coldest part of the
fridge. They should be set within 2 hours, but will
keep well overnight. **Serves 8–10.**

baked saucy **CHOC-NUT PUDDING**

A sweet and fudgy old-timer; serve hot, in syrupy scoops, over vanilla ice cream or with cream.

60 g very soft butter
125 ml (½ cup) castor sugar
1 XL free-range egg
5 ml (1 tsp) vanilla essence
250 ml (1 cup) cake flour
5 ml (1 tsp) baking powder
2 ml (½ tsp) ground cinnamon
a small pinch of sea salt
20 ml (4 tsp) cocoa powder
80 ml (⅓ cup) milk
40–50 g chopped walnuts

SAUCE
125 ml (½ cup) light brown sugar
15 ml (1 Tbsp) cocoa powder
300 ml (1⅕ cups) boiling water

Using an electric whisk, cream the butter and castor sugar until pale. Beat the egg with the vanilla essence and whisk into the butter mixture, combining to a soft, smooth consistency. Sift the flour, baking powder, cinnamon, salt and cocoa directly into the creamed mixture. Give a quick whisk to combine, then add the milk and give another quick whisk to smooth out. Fold in the walnuts and then turn the batter – which will be quite thick – into a lightly buttered 20 cm pie dish (not less than 5 cm deep, as once it's in the oven the syrup will gurgle and bubble up quite fiercely round the edges). Stir together the ingredients for the sauce and, as soon as the sugar has dissolved, pour carefully over the batter. Bake at 180 °C for 25 minutes, until risen and firm. **Serves 6.**

FRUIT flops

Even those who shy away from rich mousses always flip for flops – tropical fruit under a blanket of cream, yoghurt and a tipple of alcohol. They need to be assembled hours in advance, and then just left to do their thing in the refrigerator until dinner time. Use a bowl or goblets that are wide at the top; the cream mixture should be thick, but still pourable; and in order to soften and melt, the sugar must be sprinkled on thinly and evenly.

VERY SIMPLE FLOP

2–3 large, firm but ripe bananas, peeled and cut into small dice
fresh lemon juice
2–3 large, firm but ripe mangoes, peeled and cut into small pieces (400 g prepared weight)*
125 ml cream
a few drops of vanilla essence OR extract**
60 ml (4 Tbsp) thick low-fat Bulgarian yoghurt
15 ml (1 Tbsp) dark rum
40 ml (8 tsp) soft brown sugar

Toss the bananas in a little lemon juice, mix with the mango flesh, then spoon into four glass bowls or wide goblets, dividing equally. (Glass is preferable to pottery, so that you can see the layers.) Whip the cream with the vanilla, then fold in the yoghurt and rum. Pour over each serving of fruit, and sprinkle each with 10 ml (2 tsp) soft brown sugar (use your fingers). Refrigerate for 4–6 hours, or until the sugar just starts to melt. **Serves 4 and is easily doubled.**

* Running short of fruit, I have, on occasion, added a few chopped, canned pears. No-one noticed. Greek yoghurt may be substituted for the Bulgarian for a slightly richer topping.
** Vanilla extract is undoubtedly special in flavour, but I have found that different brands vary in quality and price, so it's a personal choice.

ELEGANT FLOP

3 large, firm but ripe mangoes, peeled and cubed (500 g prepared weight)
1 x 565 g can pitted litchis, drained, patted dry, slivered
1 large knob ginger preserve, finely chopped
1 x 175 ml tub thick Bulgarian yoghurt
30–45 ml (2–3 Tbsp) Amaretto liqueur
a few drops of vanilla essence OR extract
200 ml (⅘ cup) cream, whipped
45 ml (3 Tbsp) soft brown sugar
toasted almond flakes to decorate (or use pistachios)

Mix the prepared fruits and ginger and spoon into a large glass bowl or divide between six small bowls or goblets. Fold the yoghurt, Amaretto and vanilla into the whipped cream. Pour over the fruit to cover completely. Using your fingers, sprinkle the sugar over evenly. Refrigerate for 4–6 hours, or until the sugar starts to melt. Sprinkle with almonds before serving. **Serves 6.**

frozen CITRUS CREAMS

A type of ice cream for those of us who like the concept of home-made ices, but do not own a churn.
Refreshing, delicious, and perfectly complemented with the apricots.

LEMON

500 ml (2 cups) cream
400 ml (1⅗ cups) sifted icing sugar
20 ml (4 tsp) very finely grated lemon rind
6 XL free-range egg whites
5 ml (1 tsp) vanilla essence (or slightly less extract)

Whip the cream with the icing sugar and lemon rind until stiff. Whisk the egg whites until stiff (if you do this first you won't have to wash the beaters) and fold into the cream, with the vanilla. Use a metal spoon and fold in lightly, but combine the mixtures well. Pour into a 2-litre container and freeze quickly. Allow to soften for about 5 minutes before serving.

ORANGE

Exactly the same procedure as the lemon, but substitute 20 ml (4 tsp) very finely grated orange rind for the lemon. Walnuts are good with the orange flavour – add a handful, chopped, when folding in the egg whites.

BRANDIED APRICOT COMPOTE

Place the following in a smallish, heavy saucepan: 1 stick cinnamon; 1 star anise; 125 ml (½ cup) fresh orange juice; 125 ml (½ cup water); 2 ml (½ tsp) finely grated orange rind; 90 ml (6 Tbsp) light brown sugar. Bring to the boil, stirring to dissolve the sugar, then add 200 g soft, ready-to-eat apricots (not regular dried apricots). Reduce the heat immediately, then cover and simmer very gently for 10–12 minutes. Remove from the heat and add 30 ml (2 Tbsp) brandy and (surprisingly) a few drops of vanilla essence. Once cooled, refrigerate in a covered glass bowl for 1–2 days. Serve two or three of the plump apricots with each helping of frozen cream, with a little of the syrup spooned over. **Serves about 8.**

STRAWBERRY cheesecake pots

These are light, novel and, dressed as they are in red, they make you feel cheerful even before you dip in your spoon. Similar to cheesecake, but without any crust to interfere with the delicate flavour, and no egg yolks. Remember that the cottage/cream cheese must be at room temperature (or else the gelatine could make strings when added) and the egg whites must be at room temperature as well, or they won't whip.

250 g strawberries, rinsed and hulled
90 ml (6 Tbsp) castor sugar
1 x 250 g tub smooth, low-fat cottage cheese
12 ml (2½ tsp) gelatine
60 ml (¼ cup) water
125 ml (½ cup) cream
a few drops of vanilla essence
2 XL free-range egg whites
extra strawberries to decorate
strawberry coulis (see below) and extra cream

Slice the strawberries and place in a processor fitted with the metal blade. Add half the castor sugar and leave to stand for 10 minutes to draw the juices. Add the cottage cheese and pulse just until smoothly combined. Don't purée to a mush – the mixture should be pale pink and flecked with little bits of berries. Turn into a large bowl. Sponge the gelatine in the water, dissolve over simmering water, and slowly stir into the cheese mixture. Whip the cream with the vanilla, and fold in. Whisk the egg whites until fairly stiff, then slowly add the remaining castor sugar to make a glossy meringue mixture. Stir a spoon of this through the strawberry mixture, then fold in the remainder gently but thoroughly. Pour into eight rinsed ramekins (about 6 cm diameter, 5 cm deep) or moulds and refrigerate until set. Unmould onto individual serving plates. Decorate each with a fresh berry, pour the coulis around each little pud, and run a ribbon of the extra cream through the bright coulis. **Serves 8.**

STRAWBERRY COULIS
Blend 250 g strawberries with 30 ml (2 Tbsp) castor sugar until smoothly puréed. To spark the flavour you could add a tipple of orange liqueur, but this is optional. Makes about 350 ml (1⅖ cups).

CHERRY-AMARETTO cheesecake pots

These are similar to the Strawberry Pots, but they are not unmoulded and therefore do not require a coulis.
Use wide, tubby glasses to show off the colours; the glaze adds a glossy invitation.

2 x 250 g tubs smooth, low-fat cottage cheese
125 ml (½ cup) castor sugar
a small pinch of salt
75–90 ml (5–6 Tbsp) Amaretto liqueur
a few drops of vanilla essence
20 ml (4 tsp) gelatine
60 ml (¼ cup) water
250 ml (1 cup) cream, whipped
3 XL free-range egg whites
extra 60 ml (4 Tbsp) castor sugar

TOPPING
1 x 425 g can stoned black cherries, drained and
patted dry (reserve syrup)
2 ml (½ tsp) cornflour
60 ml (¼ cup) reserved cherry syrup
whipped cream to decorate

Whisk the cottage cheese, castor sugar, salt, liqueur and vanilla until smooth. Sponge the gelatine in the water, then dissolve over simmering water. Slowly drizzle into the cheese mixture, whisking rapidly. Fold in the whipped cream. Whisk the egg whites until peaking, then gradually add the extra castor sugar while whisking to a stiff meringue. (If you do this first, and work quickly, you won't have to wash the beaters.) Stir a spoonful of the meringue into the cheese mixture, then fold in the rest. Spoon into eight to ten ramekins (6 cm diameter, 5 cm deep) and refrigerate until set.

To prepare the topping, halve the cherries and arrange, rounded sides up, on top of each dessert. Slake the cornflour with the reserved cherry syrup, then boil for a few minutes until thick, stirring. Cool briefly, then use to glaze the cherries, using a pastry brush. Pipe rosettes of cream in the open spaces (optional) and refrigerate. **Serves 8–10.**

citrus **CUSTARD TART**

Perfect for a simple, quickly made dessert, or instead of cake for tea.

FILLING

500 ml (2 cups) milk

10 ml (2 tsp) butter

30 ml (2 Tbsp) cake flour

30 ml (2 Tbsp) cornflour

90 ml (6 Tbsp) castor sugar

a large pinch of sea salt

5 ml (1 tsp) very finely grated orange rind, or

2 ml (½ tsp) very finely grated lemon rind*

2 XL free-range eggs

5 ml (1 tsp) vanilla essence

toasted almond flakes and ground cinnamon for topping

Prepare a standard crust of fine biscuit crumbs and melted butter and press onto the base and sides of a lightly buttered pie dish, 18 cm diameter, with sloping sides – the old-fashioned glass pie dish. Bake for 10 minutes at 180 °C. Cool.

For the filling you'll need a deep, medium, heavy saucepan. Rinse with water – this helps to prevent the milk from scorching. Heat half the milk with half the butter. Meanwhile, whizz the remaining milk, the cake flour, cornflour, castor sugar, salt, orange or lemon rind and eggs in a blender until smooth. Pour into the heated milk, then stir continuously over low heat, until the mixture starts to thicken. At this stage, it's best to use a balloon whisk to achieve a smooth, lump-free custard. When it starts to pop and becomes as thick as really dense porridge, remove from the stove, beat in the remaining butter and the vanilla essence and pour onto the crust. Work quickly, as the custard firms up quickly. Spread evenly, and immediately sprinkle with the almonds and dust with cinnamon. Cool, then refrigerate before serving. **Makes 8 wedges.**

* For a taste of nostalgia, omit the citrus rinds and almonds and sprinkle the top generously with ground cinnamon to make an easy, unbaked version of *melktert*. Also add a good pinch of ground cinnamon to the crust.

litchi and amaretto **CHEESECAKE**

This cheesecake can be made ahead (without the topping) and kept in the coldest part of the fridge.

FILLING*

30 ml (2 Tbsp) gelatine
75 ml (5 Tbsp) water
3 XL free-range egg whites
200 ml (⅘ cup) castor sugar
1 x 250 g tub smooth, low-fat cottage cheese**
1 x 250 g tub cream cheese
60 ml (¼ cup) Amaretto liqueur
250 ml (1 cup) cream
5 ml (1 tsp) vanilla essence

TOPPING

1 x 565 g can pitted litchis, drained, syrup reserved
7 ml (1½ tsp) cornflour
toasted almond flakes

* All ingredients, except cream, at room temperature.
** For a slightly lower fat content, omit the cream cheese and use 2 x 250 g tubs of smooth, low-fat cottage cheese instead.

Press a regular biscuit crust onto the base only of a deep pie dish (23 cm x 6 cm). If you brush the base with a flavourless oil like canola, the slices will be easy to remove. Chill before adding the filling. Sponge the gelatine in the water, then dissolve over simmering water. Whisk the egg whites until fairly stiff, then gradually, while whisking, add half the castor sugar and whisk to a thick meringue. Without washing the beaters, whisk together the cheeses, remaining castor sugar and liqueur. When smooth, add the cream and vanilla and whip until thickened. Continue to whisk while you dribble in the dissolved gelatine. Fold in the meringue mixture, pour onto the crust and refrigerate until firm.

For the topping, pat the litchis dry, snip them into quarters and arrange on top of the cheesecake. Pour 100 ml (⅖ cup) of the reserved syrup into a small saucepan, stir in the cornflour, then bring to the boil, stirring, until clear and thick. Use a pastry brush to paint the litchis with dabs of this thick syrup – just enough to shine them up a bit. Add a sprinkling of almond flakes and return to the fridge until required.

Serves 10.

WINE-POACHED PEARS
with ginger and walnut mascarpone

Despite the title this is not a grand dessert; nevertheless, it's delicious, does not take long to make, and can be done a day ahead and kept in the refrigerator.

375 ml (1½ cups) water
125 ml (½ cup) semi-sweet white wine
125 ml (½ cup) sugar
4 large, firm, unblemished pears (about 800 g),
Packham's or Beurre Bosc are good choices
fresh lemon juice (optional)
ground cinnamon

Mix the water, wine and sugar in a large frying pan and heat slowly, stirring now and then to dissolve the sugar. When you're not stirring, peel, halve and core the pears, then place in the bubbling syrup, rounded sides up. They should fit the pan snugly. Reduce the heat to very low and simmer gently for 30 minutes or until soft but still perfectly shaped; test with a sharp skewer. If done, use a slotted spoon to arrange the pears, rounded sides still up, in a shallow serving dish – a 23 cm pie dish is just right. Taste the syrup in the pan, and if too sweet, add a dash of lemon juice. Increase the heat and boil, uncovered, until bubbly and syrupy – a matter of minutes. Pour over the pears, dust lightly with cinnamon, cool, then cover and refrigerate. **Makes at least 4 plump servings.**

GINGER AND WALNUT MASCARPONE
125 g mascarpone
a few drops of vanilla essence
15 ml (1 Tbsp) sifted icing sugar
15 ml (1 Tbsp) milk
45 ml (3 Tbsp) chopped walnuts
30–45 ml (2–3 Tbsp) finely chopped ginger preserve

Whisk the mascarpone, vanilla essence, icing sugar and milk with an electric hand-held whisk. This takes longer to get results than whipping cream, but it does whip up a lighter mascarpone with increased volume. Fold in the walnuts and ginger and refrigerate. Serve one or two pear halves per diner with a dollop of mascarpone at the side, or enlarge the hollows and pile with mascarpone.

PEARS IN PHYLLO BASKETS
with sabayon

Baked custard has its place, but there are times when you want to impress with a dessert that is a little smarter. Then this is it. The title may sound daunting, but the baskets are optional and no step is either difficult or time-consuming.

about 750 g slightly underripe Packham's Triumph pears
200 ml (⅘ cup) water
100 ml (⅖ cup) sugar
1 stick cinnamon
10 ml (2 tsp) fresh lemon juice
toasted almond flakes to decorate

SABAYON
3 XL free-range egg yolks
75 ml (5 Tbsp) sugar
5 ml (1 tsp) cornflour
45 ml (3 Tbsp) Amaretto liqueur
125 ml (½ cup) cream

Peel, halve and core the pears. Bring the water, sugar, cinnamon and lemon juice to the boil in a wide-based pan, add the pears in a single layer, rounded sides up, cover and poach gently just until soft. Cool in the poaching liquid, then drain and chill. To make the sabayon, put the egg yolks, sugar and cornflour in the top of a small double boiler, or into a small saucepan set on top of a larger one, and, using a balloon whisk, whisk until pale and thick. Keep the water simmering, not boiling, or the mixture will scramble; however, it should not be undercooked either, or it will separate on standing. (This is the only tricky part.) Now slowly add the liqueur, and, using a wooden spoon, stir until the mixture thickens again – it should be creamy and butterscotch-coloured. Pour into a small container, cool, then refrigerate. Just before serving, whip the cream and fold it in. To serve, place one pear half, rounded side up, on each serving plate, or nestle it in a phyllo basket. Pour over enough of the sabayon to coat, sprinkle with almonds, and serve at once. **The sabayon is enough for 10–12 small pear halves.**

PHYLLO BASKETS (OPTIONAL)
Brush large, deep muffin tins with butter. Press in a square of phyllo, using only one layer. Brush lightly with melted butter, top with another square and brush with a little more butter. Bake at 200 °C for 5 minutes, until browned, then lift out of the tins and cool on a rack. You can neaten the edges by snipping with kitchen scissors.

cinnamon-poached
PEARS WITH NUT LIQUEUR

A memorable dessert, this one, supremely elegant and yet so easy to prepare – plus there are options: you can use either Amaretto and almonds, or Frangelico and hazelnuts; you can serve the pears plain to relish the fine flavours; with crème fraîche to offset the sweetness; or with a blob of mascarpone piled into the hollows. Very special, any which way.

4 large pears (700–800 g), unblemished and not quite ripe
fresh lemon juice
500 ml (2 cups) water
125 ml (½ cup) sugar
2 fat sticks cinnamon
45–60 ml (3–4 Tbsp) Amaretto OR Frangelico liqueur
toasted almonds OR roasted hazelnuts*, coarsely crushed

Peel the pears as smoothly as possible, halve, and nick out the pips and core. Brush the rounded sides with lemon juice. Bring the water, sugar and cinnamon to the boil in a wide-based frying pan. Add the pears, rounded sides up, in a single layer. Cover and simmer gently for about 30 minutes. Test with the tip of a skewer – they should be soft but definitely not mushy. Using a slotted spoon, remove the pears from the poaching liquid and arrange them in a shallow dish to fit snugly, rounded sides up. Discard the cinnamon. Turn up the heat and boil the poaching liquid rapidly, uncovered, for 10–12 minutes, or until very bubbly, a pale toffee colour, and reduced to about 150 ml (⅔ cup). Remove from the stove, stir in the chosen liqueur, and slowly pour the syrup over the pears. Leave to cool, basting a few times, then cover and refrigerate for a few hours. Sprinkle with the nuts before serving. **Serves 4–8.**

* If using hazelnuts, remove the loose skins after roasting by rubbing the nuts in a clean kitchen towel.

BAKING

lemon and almond **SHORTBREAD SQUARES**

Melt-in-the-mouth, buttery shortbread is a perennially popular tea-time favourite. Traditionally made with only four ingredients, but in the following recipes I have introduced some unusual new flavours.

250 g butter (at room temperature), cubed
finely grated rind of 1 large lemon
125 ml (½ cup) castor sugar
600 ml (2⅖ cups) cake flour
150 ml (⅗ cup) cornflour*
60–75 ml (4–5 Tbsp) flaked almonds, lightly toasted
about 5 ml (1 tsp) castor sugar for dusting

Place the butter and lemon rind in a large mixing bowl. (Use a big, thick-skinned, well-washed lemon, and be careful not to include any of the pith when grating.) Using an electric whisk, cream these well, then slowly beat in the castor sugar until the mixture is fluffy and pale yellow. Sift the flour with the cornflour and add gradually, beating well, until the mixture is moist and finely crumbed, then use your hands to knead until the mixture comes together in a smooth, putty-like ball. Finally, knead in the almonds. Line a 26 x 20 cm** baking sheet with baking paper, and press the mixture in firmly and as evenly as possible. Use a fork to prick the mixture all over, and mark lightly into squares. Bake on the middle shelf of the oven at 160 °C for 10 minutes, then reduce the heat to 150 °C and bake for a further 50 minutes. When done, the shortbread should be a rich blonde colour, never browned. Remove from the oven and carefully cut through the squares. Sprinkle with castor sugar, then leave on the sheet until absolutely cold before removing. **Makes about 20 squares, depending on size.**

* Rice flour is traditional, but not readily available in South Africa – cornflour makes a good substitute.
** The size of the baking sheet is important – no larger, or the shortbread will be too thin.

rosemary SHORTBREAD FINGERS

This is a rich shortbread, crisp and addictive, with a fragrant surprise in the flavour.
The recipe makes a large batch.

750 ml (3 cups) cake flour
125 ml (½ cup) rice flour*
250 g very soft butter
125 ml (½ cup) castor sugar
15 ml (1 Tbsp) very finely chopped fresh rosemary leaves

Sift the two flours together. Using an electric whisk, cream the butter very well. Slowly beat in the sugar, and whisk until the mixture becomes pale and fluffy, then gradually add the flour. Whisk until it all becomes very moist and crumbly. Mix in the rosemary and then, using your hands, knead for a few minutes before shaping into a soft, smooth ball. Line a 25 x 20 cm tin with baking paper (even if it is a non-stick pan). Secure the baking paper at the corners with a dab of oil. Place the ball of dough in the tin and, pressing down firmly, spread it out into the corners. Continue to press down hard until the mixture is smoothly and evenly spread. Prick well all over and mark lightly into 28 fingers. Bake at 150 °C for 50–55 minutes until very pale beige and firm.

Remove from the oven and cut through the markings, but leave in the tin until cold. Sprinkle with a drizzle of castor sugar, lift out carefully, and store in an airtight container. **Makes 28.**

* Cornflour can be used instead.

FARMHOUSE FINGER RUSKS with buttermilk and oats

This version is good and wholesome – the soft, sticky dough is simply turned into a loaf tin
(for a loaf of rusks) or a rectangular tin (for a flattish slab). Once baked, cool, turn out, and cut into fingers.
You can make them with white flour, bran-rich flour, or half white and half bran-rich,
or in any proportion you like, as long as the total is 500 g.

500 g self-raising flour
5 ml (1 tsp) salt
5 ml (1 tsp) baking powder
250 ml (1 cup) sugar
500 ml (2 cups) porridge oats
75 ml (5 Tbsp) currants (optional)
125 g butter, melted
2 large free-range eggs
about 250 ml (1 cup) buttermilk
90 ml (6 Tbsp) oil

Sift the flour, salt and baking powder into a bowl.
If using bran-rich flour, add the bran left in the sieve.
Mix in the sugar, oats and currants, then mix in the
melted butter. In a separate bowl, whisk the eggs,
buttermilk and oil and add to the flour mixture.
Combine well; the dough should be squishy and
soft. If using a lot of bran-rich flour, you will need
a little extra buttermilk. Turn the dough into either a
26 x 9 x 7 cm loaf tin, oiled and then lined (base and
sides) with baking paper, or a 20 x 26 cm baking tin,
lined in the same way. In both cases, spread evenly,
levelling the top with a dampened hand and a wet
wooden spoon. Bake the rectangular batch at 180 °C
for 45 minutes. The loaf tin, being deeper, will take
1 hour. Cool before turning out. For perfect finger
shapes, cut off the crusty sides before cutting across
into thick slices and then into fingers. Arrange on
baking sheets lined with several layers of baking
paper (as the rusks tend to brown quickly) and dry
out in a very low oven, about 100 °C, for several
hours, turning once. When dry, leave to cool in the
oven before storing. **Makes dozens, depending
on how thick and short or long and thinly you slice
the fingers.**

ouma's aniseed **BUTTERMILK RUSKS**

The favourite, old-fashioned, morning coffee dunk, neither too sweet nor buttery for so early in the day.

500 g self-raising flour
5 ml (1 tsp) salt
2 ml (½ tsp) baking powder
125 ml (½ cup) sugar
10 ml (2 tsp) aniseed, coarsely crushed with a rolling pin
125 g soft butter
1 XL free-range egg
200 ml (⅘ cup) buttermilk

Sift the flour, salt and baking powder into a large bowl, then mix in the sugar and aniseed. Rub in the butter until finely crumbled. Or melt the butter, which is quicker and works just as well, and mix into the flour mixture before adding the remaining ingredients. Whisk the egg into the buttermilk, pour into the flour mixture, mix well and then start to knead. The more you knead, the better the rusks will rise. If the dough becomes sticky (which is unlikely), flour your hands as necessary; if too dry, add a drop more buttermilk, but be careful of making too soft a dough. Continue kneading until it forms a smooth, elastic ball and leaves the sides of the bowl clean. Break off eight equal pieces and work each one into a smooth, round ball. Place the balls up against each other in a medium-sized loaf tin (20 x 10 x 7 cm is just right) first brushed with oil and then lined, base and sides, with baking paper. Bake at 200 °C for 20 minutes, then at 180 °C for 30 minutes; test by poking a skewer into the centre. Leave to stand for 10 minutes before turning out onto a rack; remove paper, and leave until cool enough to handle. Break the balls apart, and then, with the help of a knife, nick and break open again – try not to cut right through, just here and there, and then break into rusk shapes. Place in a single layer on a baking sheet lined with several sheets of baking paper, and dry out in a very low oven, about 100 °C, turning once.
Makes about 32, depending on size.

honeyed **GINGER COOKIES**

Very moreish caramel-coloured chews, made with really basic ingredients. These are not hard, dunking-type biscuits, but fairly soft with an addictive flavour.

250 ml (1 cup) cake flour
15 ml (1 Tbsp) ground ginger
a pinch of salt
1 ml (¼ tsp) ground cinnamon
125 ml (½ cup) light brown sugar
125 ml (½ cup) wholewheat flour
125 g soft butter
5 ml (1 tsp) bicarbonate of soda
15 ml (1 Tbsp) honey
30 ml (2 Tbsp) hot water

Sift the cake flour, ginger, salt and cinnamon. Add the sugar and wholewheat flour. Mix in the butter, whisking until the mixture resembles fine crumbs. Mix the bicarb and honey into the water and, when melted, whisk into the flour mixture. Mix well – the mixture will be very soft. Shape into a ball, pinch off pieces, roll into balls and place on baking sheets that have been first oiled and then lined with two sheets* of baking paper, leaving room for spreading. Press down with a fork, and bake at 180 °C for 18–20 minutes until a rich caramel colour. Using a spatula, carefully remove to a rack to cool. **Makes 20.**

* With ovens that heat from below, biscuits easily get overbrowned bottoms. Lining baking trays with a double layer of baking paper usually prevents this.

ALMOND BISCOTTI with cherries and amaretto

Not quite a rusk, not quite a biscuit, but crisp little things to dunk into coffee or sweet wine after a meal.
I toast the almonds for added flavour, and use Amaretto instead of artificial almond essence.

3 large free-range eggs
200 ml (⅘ cup) castor sugar
2 ml (½ tsp) vanilla essence
30 ml (2 Tbsp) Amaretto liqueur
750 ml (3 cups) cake flour
a pinch of sea salt
5 ml (1 tsp) baking powder
2 ml (½ tsp) freshly grated nutmeg
100 g blanched almonds, whole, slivered or flaked, toasted
12 glacé cherries, rinsed, dried and chopped

Whisk the eggs, castor sugar, vanilla essence and liqueur very well, until light and creamy. Sift in the flour, salt, baking powder and nutmeg. Using an electric whisk, mix to a soft dough, then gather up and work into a smooth ball with your hands. Place on a lightly floured board. Roll the dough (flouring your hands occasionally, as it can be sticky) into a log, incorporating the nuts and cherries as you go. (If you don't like cherries, leave them out – I add them for their cheerful colour.) The almonds I use are usually the flaked ones, as it is easier to spread them throughout the dough so that in the end each slice contains a few pieces. When all the nuts and cherries are incorporated, divide into two logs, each about 24 cm long and 5 cm wide. Lightly oil a large baking sheet and cover the base with baking paper. Place the logs side by side, but apart, as they will puff up in the oven, and flatten gently with your palm. Bake at 160 °C for 30 minutes, until deep cream in colour. Remove from the oven and leave to stand for 5 minutes. Reduce temperature to 140 °C, slice off the pointy ends of the logs, then slice the rest into diagonal 1 cm thick slices. Place flat on the sheet and bake for 20 minutes. Turn and bake for a further 20–30 minutes until dry and just beginning to look toasted. Cool on the baking sheet before storing in an airtight container. **Makes 40.**

jumbo **OAT CRISPS**

Big as small saucers, flat, crunchy and wholesome, these are best made in relays because they spread with such abandon.

125 g very soft butter
125 ml (½ cup) oil
250 ml (1 cup) sugar
250 ml (1 cup) oats
250 ml (1 cup) wholewheat flour
125 ml (½ cup) cake flour
125 ml (½ cup) desiccated coconut
a pinch of salt
5 ml (1 tsp) bicarbonate of soda
15 ml (1 Tbsp) hot water
45–60 ml (3–4 Tbsp) currants
60 ml (4 Tbsp) sunflower seeds
5 ml (1 tsp) vanilla essence

Whisk together the butter, oil, sugar, oats, both flours, coconut and salt, combining well to make a soft dough. Dissolve the bicarbonate of soda in the hot water and add, mixing well, then mix in the currants, sunflower seeds and vanilla essence. Shape the mixture into a ball with your hands, then pinch off pieces and shape into flat patties by tossing between your palms. The dough is very sticky, and this is the best way to handle it. Place the patties on oiled, double-lined baking sheets, leaving plenty of room for spreading. Press down lightly with a fork, and bake at 180 °C for 15 minutes until they have grown into large, flat, golden-brown discs. As they will be very soft, leave on the trays to crisp for a few minutes, then use a spatula to remove to cooling racks. **Make a minimum of 21 – or more, if you prefer to make smaller crisps.**

butter **PECAN SNAPS**

A rich, crunchy picture-book cookie, which will be appreciated by cooks who have no time to roll out, chill, cut or even decorate. Using a hand-held electric whisk further simplifies preparation.

250 g soft butter
250 ml (1 cup) castor sugar
1 large free-range egg, beaten
5 ml (1 tsp) vanilla essence
750 ml (3 cups) flour – white bread flour, or cake flour,
or half and half
5 ml (1 tsp) bicarbonate of soda
5 ml (1 tsp) ground cinnamon
2 ml (½ tsp) freshly grated nutmeg
a pinch of sea salt
100 g pecan nuts, chopped

Cream the butter and castor sugar until light and pale. Beat in the egg and vanilla essence. Sift in, all together, the flour, bicarb, spices and salt, and whisk to make a soft dough. Add the pecans and, using your hands, work the mixture into a ball. Pinch off pieces and roll into fairly large marbles – the dough is very soft and it will be necessary to flour your hands now and then. Place well apart on baking sheets, first oiled and then lined with two layers of baking paper. Flatten lightly with a fork, and bake at 160 °C for 18–20 minutes until the cookies have spread into discs and are just beginning to brown round the edges. Use a spatula to transfer to a rack to cool. **Makes 48.**

fruity CUPCAKES

These look like brown muffins, but they're not. Based on a carrot cake mixture, they're dense with fruit and spices and, topped with butter icing*, they make perfect, single-serving little cakes.

2 large free-range eggs
125 ml (½ cup) light brown sugar
125 ml (½ cup) oil
250 ml (1 cup) flour – cake flour, white bread flour,
   or brown flour (not wholewheat)
2 ml (½ tsp) bicarbonate of soda
5 ml (1 tsp) baking powder
a tiny pinch of sea salt
2 ml (½ tsp) ground cinnamon
1 ml (¼ tsp) ground mixed spice
125 ml (½ cup) dried fruit cake mix
60 ml (4 Tbsp) finely chopped, pitted dates
2 medium or 1 jumbo carrot, coarsely grated (125 g)
60 ml (4 Tbsp) chopped walnuts
2 ml (½ tsp) vanilla essence
white butter icing and walnut halves for topping

Whisk the eggs and sugar. Add the oil and whisk well until the mixture is creamy and pale butterscotch in colour. Sift the dry ingredients – you can sift them straight into the creamed mixture (if using brown flour, add any bran left in the sieve). Combine well, then stir in the fruit mix, dates, carrot, nuts and essence. Have a muffin tin ready and waiting – you'll need a large one, to take 10 paper cups (the big cups with a base diameter of 4 cm) – one cup in each hollow. Fill each cup to two-thirds full. Bake at 160 °C for 30–35 minutes until richly browned and well risen; test with a skewer, it should come out clean when they're done. (Note that these cakes do not peak, but have smooth, rounded tops.) Leave to cool in the pan before lifting out in their paper cases. Top each with a small blob of icing, smooth over with a damp spatula (don't be too concerned about wavy edges, they must look homespun) and lightly press in the halved nuts. **Makes 10.**

* If preferred, you could forget the icing, and top each with a nut before baking. Also good, and less sweet.

plain **GOLDEN SCONES**

Serve freshly baked, with butter, jam and cream. Follow the baking instructions carefully, never twist when cutting them out, and don't omit the lemon juice, which helps to lighten the scones.

500 ml (2 cups) cake flour
20 ml (4 tsp) baking powder
1 ml (¼ tsp) sea salt
30 ml (2 Tbsp) castor sugar
1 large free-range egg
60 ml (¼ cup) each oil, milk and water
5 ml (1 tsp) fresh lemon juice
beaten egg or milk to glaze

Sift the dry ingredients into a mixing bowl. Whisk together the egg, oil, milk, water and lemon juice. Add to the sifted mixture and mix lightly, using a firm spatula and then, using your hands, quickly shape into a soft ball – flouring your hands if necessary. Pat out into a 2 cm thick circle or rectangle on a lightly floured board; don't be heavy-handed, but the dough needs to be given a quick knead and smoothing out to remove any surface cracks. Cut out, using either a 6 cm round cutter, flouring it after every second scone, or cut into squares with a floured knife. Gather up any offcuts and pat out smoothly again to give you eight scones in total. Place fairly close together, but not quite touching, on a baking sheet lined with baking paper. Brush the tops with egg or milk, and bake near the top of the oven at 220 °C for 15 minutes until well risen and golden. Remove to a rack to cool down before serving. Scones should be carefully broken in half, not cut, before spreading. **Makes 8.**

rosemary-buttermilk **SCONES**

Plump, savoury scones topped with melted cheese – these are delicious served freshly baked with morning coffee, with brunch, or with soup. Switch on the oven, snip the herbs, and then they're made in less time than they take to bake.

500 ml (2 cups) self-raising flour*
1 ml (¼ tsp) salt
15 ml (1 Tbsp) castor sugar
15 ml (1 Tbsp) finely chopped fresh rosemary leaves
15 ml (1 Tbsp) snipped fresh chives
1 XL free-range egg
60 ml (¼ cup) oil
buttermilk
milk and finely grated Cheddar cheese for topping

Sift the flour, salt and castor sugar and mix in the herbs. Break the egg into a measuring jug, add the oil and enough buttermilk to reach the 200 ml (⅘ cup) mark – about 125 ml (½ cup) buttermilk should just do it. Whisk these together, then add to the dry ingredients. Using a fork, mix quickly until the dough holds together, then use your hands to form into a ball. Pat out, 2 cm thick, on a lightly floured board and use a 5 cm scone cutter to cut into rounds – don't twist when cutting. Place, almost touching, on a baking tray lined with baking paper, brush the tops lightly with milk and sprinkle with cheese. Bake at 220 °C just above the centre of the oven for about 14 minutes until the scones have ballooned beautifully, are golden in colour and the cheese has melted. **Makes 10.**

* For a more wholesome scone, substitute bran-rich self-raising flour in any ratio preferred, remembering that the bran will require slightly more liquid.

BUTTERMILK MUFFINS with cheese and sun-dried tomatoes

Bake, break and serve warm with butter and an eggy dish, or with soup, or for elevenses with coffee instead of something sweet.

500 ml (2 cups) bran-rich self-raising flour (or use white self-raising, or half and half)
2 ml (½ tsp) mustard powder
2 ml (½ tsp) salt
10 ml (2 tsp) castor sugar
2 pickling onions, coarsely grated
2 ml (½ tsp) dried mixed herbs
90 ml (6 Tbsp) finely snipped sun-dried tomatoes (first drained on kitchen paper if in oil)
60 g Cheddar cheese, grated
60 ml (4 Tbsp) finely chopped fresh parsley
1 XL free-range egg
250 ml (1 cup) buttermilk
60 ml (¼ cup) oil
about 50 g extra Cheddar cheese, and paprika for topping

Sift the flour, mustard powder, salt and castor sugar into a mixing bowl, adding any bran left in the sieve. Mix in the onions, dried herbs, tomatoes, cheese and parsley. Whisk together the egg, buttermilk and oil. Make a well in the dry ingredients and pour in the liquid. Stir quickly and lightly until the ingredients are just combined – do not try to smooth the batter, it should be lumpy. Spoon into 10 large, lightly oiled hollows in a muffin pan (not paper cups), dividing equally. Top generously with extra grated cheese, dust with paprika and bake immediately at 200 °C for 25 minutes, until risen and golden brown. Place on a rack to cool briefly before gently removing the muffins. **Makes 10.**

brown buttermilk **MUFFINS**

... with raisins and spice and a touch of orange, all of which combine to make these a great choice
to serve at a brunch, with butter and lime marmalade.

250 ml (1 cup) cake flour

a large pinch of salt

5 ml (1 tsp) bicarbonate of soda

2 ml (½ tsp) ground mixed spice

60 ml (4 Tbsp) light brown sugar

250 ml (1 cup) wholewheat flour

200 ml (⅘ cup) seedless raisins

1 XL free-range egg

60 ml (¼ cup) oil

60 ml (¼ cup) runny honey or golden syrup

250 ml (1 cup) buttermilk

5 ml (1 tsp) very finely grated orange rind

Sift together the flour, salt, bicarb and spice.
Mix in the sugar, wholewheat flour and raisins.
Whisk together the egg, oil, honey or syrup,
buttermilk and orange rind and add this mixture
to the dry ingredients; mix quickly to a lumpy batter.
Spoon into large, lightly oiled muffin cups (not paper
cups), filling them to the three-quarter level, and
bake on the middle shelf of the oven at 180 °C for
25 minutes – do the skewer test and, if done, leave
to stand for a few minutes before removing to a rack
to cool. **Makes 10 fat muffins.**

fruitcake **MUFFINS**

Dark and knobbly, sweet and spicy muffins. No need to butter these, they are moist enough to enjoy just as they are, and they're a useful bake when the hens are off the lay – no eggs.

250 ml (1 cup) dried fruit cake mix
75 g butter, diced
250 ml (1 cup) boiling water
375 ml (1½ cups) cake flour*
5 ml (1 tsp) baking powder
5 ml (1 tsp) bicarbonate of soda
a pinch of salt
7 ml (1½ tsp) ground cinnamon
2 ml (½ tsp) freshly grated nutmeg
125 ml (½ cup) wholewheat flour
125 ml (½ cup) light brown sugar
30 g pecans, chopped
5 ml (1 tsp) vanilla essence

* White bread flour can replace the cake flour and, for a more wholesome muffin, 250 ml (1 cup) wholewheat and 250 ml (1 cup) cake or white bread flour may be used instead of the given ratios.

Place the fruit mix and butter in a bowl, pour the boiling water over, stir to melt the butter and leave to cool for about 15 minutes. Sift the flour, baking powder, bicarb, salt and spices, mix in the wholewheat flour, sugar and pecans, then pour the fruit mixture into a well in the centre of the dry ingredients. Add the vanilla and mix very quickly to a lumpy batter – mix only until no trace of flour remains – then spoon into large, lightly oiled muffin cups (not paper cups), filling each to the three-quarter level. Bake on the middle shelf of the oven at 180 °C for 20 minutes until brown and firm – test with a skewer to check whether they are cooked through. Leave to stand a few minutes before removing to a rack to cool. **Makes 9 large muffins.**

lemon, nut and semolina **SLAB CAKE**

The thick batter is spread thinly in a large tin, drenched in syrup once baked, showered with lemon peel, left to fatten up a bit, and then cut into squares to serve.

125 g soft butter

90 ml (6 Tbsp) castor sugar

10 ml (2 tsp) finely grated lemon rind

4 XL free-range eggs, separated

250 ml (1 cup) semolina

125 ml (½ cup) cake flour

7 ml (1½ tsp) ground cinnamon

a small pinch of salt

7 ml (1½ tsp) baking powder

100 ml (⅖ cup) milk

5 ml (1 tsp) vanilla essence

50 g walnuts, chopped

SYRUP

peel of 2 large lemons, slivered into thin, short shreds

200 ml (⅘ cup) sugar

250 ml (1 cup) water

15 ml (1 Tbsp) fresh lemon juice

15 ml (1 Tbsp) Limetto Cinzano (optional – tasting
  of lemon and lime, it adds a smart touch)

Cream the butter, sugar and lemon rind. Whisk in the yolks, singly, then mix in the semolina. Sift in the remaining dry ingredients and stir – the mixture will be thick. Mix in the milk and vanilla essence and fold in the stiffly beaten egg whites and the nuts. The mixture may appear slightly curdled, but should smooth out. Spread levelly into a 26 x 20 cm tin lined with baking paper (base and sides), and bake on the middle shelf at 180 °C for 25 minutes until pale brown, slightly risen and firm.

Prepare the syrup while the cake is baking. Place the lemon shreds in a heavy saucepan and add the sugar, water and lemon juice. Bring to the boil, stirring to dissolve the sugar, then leave to bubble for 5 minutes until syrupy and reduced. Remove and add the Limetto. Remove the cake from the oven, prick, and drizzle with the warm syrup, making sure the lemon peel doesn't clump. Cool in the tin, then cut into 18–20 pieces. Eat it within 3 days, it will not keep for longer. **Makes 18–20 squares.**

nutty as a fruitcake **FRUITCAKE**

Heavy with fruit, nuts and cherries, it weighs 1–1.5 kg and, as it is not a very thick cake, it can take a layer of marzipan and icing to become a last-minute Christmas cake. If you would rather have it plain, the mixture is stiff enough to support halved cherries, decoratively arranged on the top before baking. If you want a deeper, 'fatter' cake, use a 20 cm round tin, but bake for slightly longer.

500 g dried fruit cake mix
250 ml (1 cup) seedless raisins
125 ml (½ cup) light brown sugar
125 ml (½ cup) white sugar
5 ml (1 tsp) bicarbonate of soda
125 g butter, roughly cubed
250 ml (1 cup) water
2 XL free-range eggs
5 ml (1 tsp) vanilla essence
15 ml (1 Tbsp) dark rum
30 ml (2 Tbsp) brandy
500 ml (2 cups) cake flour
10 ml (2 tsp) baking powder
a pinch of salt
2 ml (½ tsp) each ground cinnamon, mixed spice and freshly grated nutmeg
50 g glacé cherries, chopped
50 g walnuts, coarsely chopped
15 ml (1 Tbsp) finely chopped ginger preserve

Bring the cake mixture, raisins, both sugars, bicarb, butter and water to the boil in a large, deep saucepan – it must be deep as the bicarb froths up. Stir and reduce the heat to low, then half-cover and simmer for 15 minutes until the liquid is absorbed. Cool completely before proceeding. Whisk together the eggs, vanilla, rum and brandy. Add to the fruit mixture (in a large bowl), then sift in the flour, baking powder, salt and spices. Mix well, then add the cherries, walnuts and ginger. Turn this thick, sticky mixture into a 21 x 6 cm deep, round cake tin, base and sides lined with baking paper. Smooth the top and arrange halved cherries on top, if using. Bake at 160 °C for 1 hour 10 minutes; test with a skewer in the centre of the cake – it should come out clean. Cool in the tin before turning out. Store in an airtight container for a day or two before enjoying.
Makes 1 large cake.

chocolate-glazed **DEVIL'S FOOD CAKE**

Serve as is for a special tea, or for a rich treat of a dessert serve slices with a dollop of crème fraîche alongside and a small tumble of berries.

375 ml (1½ cups) cake flour
125 ml (½ cup) cocoa powder
5 ml (1 tsp) bicarbonate of soda
2 ml (½ tsp) baking powder
5 ml (1 tsp) ground cinnamon
250 ml (1 cup) castor sugar
125 g butter
7 ml (1½ tsp) instant coffee granules
250 ml (1 cup) buttermilk
2 XL free-range eggs
7 ml (1½ tsp) vanilla essence

GANACHE
150 g dark chocolate (use hard chocolate, such as Bournville or Albany), broken into pieces
125 ml (½ cup) cream
22 ml (1½ Tbsp) sifted icing sugar

Sift the flour, cocoa, bicarb, baking powder, cinnamon and castor sugar into a mixing bowl. Melt the butter over low heat with the coffee and, when dissolved, add to the dry ingredients together with 125 ml (½ cup) of the buttermilk. Using an electric whisk, beat on low speed for 1–2 minutes until combined – the mixture will be thick. Beat the remaining buttermilk with the eggs and vanilla and add to the flour mixture. Now whisk at high speed for 1½ minutes until the mixture is very smooth and somewhat lighter in colour. Turn into a deep, 20 cm layer cake tin, bottom and sides lined with baking paper. Use a spatula to level the top gently, and then bake on the middle shelf of the oven at 180 °C for 55–60 minutes. It will rise dramatically while in the oven, but settles down once baked. If a skewer inserted into the middle of the cake comes out dry, it's done. Remove from the oven and leave to cool in the tin. Turn out when cold, and place base (flat) side up on a serving plate.

To make the ganache, smear a small saucepan with butter and add the chocolate and the cream. Melt over low heat, then stir in the icing sugar. Remove from the stove as soon as the mixture is smooth, and slowly drizzle it over the top of the cake. Use a spatula to smooth it out to the edges – it should cover the top completely – then leave to set. This will take several hours, and the cake should only be cut after a day.

chocolate-orange LAYER CAKE

A large, dark cake. The ingredients are basic, it's easy to make and the flavour is super.

90 ml (6 Tbsp) cocoa powder
5 ml (1 tsp) instant coffee granules
250 ml (1 cup) boiling water
10 ml (2 tsp) finely grated orange rind*
4 XL free-range eggs, separated
375 ml (1½ cups) castor sugar
5 ml (1 tsp) vanilla essence
125 ml (½ cup) oil
500 ml (2 cups) cake flour
15 ml (1 Tbsp) baking powder
a pinch of salt

Mix the cocoa, coffee, water and orange rind, then leave to cool. Whisk the egg yolks with the castor sugar and vanilla until the sugar has dissolved and the mixture resembles creamy butter. Add the cocoa mixture and oil, and whisk until combined. Sift in the flour, baking powder and salt, and whisk briefly, just until smooth. Fold in the stiffly whisked egg whites, using a metal spoon, then pour into two 20 cm round cake tins, first brushed with oil, then base and sides lined with baking paper. Bake on the middle shelf of the oven at 180 °C for about 25 minutes – do the skewer test. Leave to stand for a few minutes before inverting onto a rack. Remove the baking paper and cool, then ice (see below) and decorate with chocolate scrolls or as preferred.

VANILLA BUTTER ICING
Whisk the following together until smooth:
750 ml (3 cups) icing sugar, sifted; 30 ml (2 Tbsp) cocoa powder; 60 ml (4 Tbsp) softened butter; 5 ml (1 tsp) instant coffee granules dissolved in 30 ml (2 Tbsp) cold water; 5 ml (1 tsp) vanilla essence; a little milk to moisten.

* When using orange rind to flavour cakes, biscuits or desserts, use firm but ripe oranges and a very fine grater – the result will be almost a pulp, and a little will provide plenty of flavour. Wash the oranges in hot water first to get rid of the waxy coating.

coffee and spice **LAYER CAKE**

Despite the popular invasion of croissants and preserves, baguettes, goat's cheese and blueberry muffins with mascarpone, there's still a place, now and then, for one of those imposing iced layer cakes that used to be seen on every tea table some time in the past. Here's a reminder.

30 ml (2 Tbsp) instant coffee granules
250 ml (1 cup) hot water
125 ml (½ cup) oil
4 XL free-range eggs, beaten
5 ml (1 tsp) vanilla essence
500 ml (2 cups) cake flour
15 ml (1 Tbsp) baking powder
2 ml (½ tsp) ground mixed spice
5 ml (1 tsp) ground cinnamon
30 ml (2 Tbsp) cornflour
275 ml (1 cup plus 5 tsp) castor sugar
a pinch of salt
4 XL free-range egg whites, beaten until stiff

Dissolve the coffee granules in the hot water, then leave to cool completely. Add the oil, beaten eggs and vanilla and whisk to combine. Sift the flour, baking powder, spices, cornflour, castor sugar and salt into a large mixing bowl, add the coffee mixture, and whisk quickly just until smoothly combined – do not overbeat. Using a metal spoon, fold in the egg whites in two batches. (Whisk these right at the start, and then you won't have to wash the beaters.) Turn into two 20 cm round cake tins, first brushed with oil, then base and sides lined with baking paper, and bake on the middle shelf of the oven at 180 °C for 30 minutes. Leave to stand for a few minutes before turning onto a rack to cool, and remove the baking paper. Ice as suggested below.

COFFEE BUTTER ICING

To sandwich the layers and cover the top thickly, you'll need to mix together: 90 g soft butter; 750 ml (3 cups) sifted icing sugar; 5 ml (1 tsp) instant coffee granules dissolved in 15 ml (1 Tbsp) water; 2 ml (½ tsp) vanilla essence and about 15 ml (1 Tbsp) milk. Pecan nuts are optional, but they look very good on a coffee cake.

brown DOUBLE-GINGER LOAF

If you love ginger, this is for you: it's not gingerbread as such, but a large, perfumed loaf which is delicious served sliced with soft goat's cheese (like cylinders of chevin) or cream cheese, and a preserve such as kumquat or grapefruit on the side. An unusual treat at a brunch or tea.

125 g soft butter
200 ml (⅘ cup) castor sugar
1 XL free-range egg, lightly beaten
1 knob fresh root ginger, peeled and coarsely grated
(about 15 ml (1 Tbsp))
45 ml (3 Tbsp) runny honey
45 ml (3 Tbsp) golden syrup
625 ml (2½ cups) cake flour*
15 ml (1 Tbsp) ground ginger
5 ml (1 tsp) bicarbonate of soda
5 ml (1 tsp) baking powder
2 ml (½ tsp) ground mixed spice
200 ml (⅘ cup) milk
5 ml (1 tsp) vanilla essence
icing sugar for dusting (optional)

* If preferred, use half cake flour and half brown flour – brown flour adds an extra fillip of fibre, but it does make a slightly heavier and less moist loaf.

Using an electric whisk, cream the butter and castor sugar until light and fluffy. Whisk in the egg, then mix in the grated ginger, honey and syrup. Beat until thick and creamy. Sift the flour, ground ginger, bicarb, baking powder and mixed spice. Whisk this into the creamed mixture, alternately with the milk, beginning and ending with the flour mixture, and mix to a fairly stiff batter. Finally add the vanilla. Turn into a 26 x 9 x 7 cm loaf tin, oiled and then lined, base and sides, with baking paper. (Oiling the tin first allows the paper to adhere.) For a dumpier loaf, use a 20 x 9 x 7 cm tin. Bake at 160 °C for 1¼ hours until caramel brown, risen and firm – test with a skewer. Leave to stand for a few minutes before turning out onto a rack, remove baking paper and cool. Dust with icing sugar before slicing.
Makes 1 large loaf.

fruit and carrot **LOAF**

A sweet, dense brown loaf. Serve sliced and buttered.

125 g dried fruit cake mix

300 ml (1⅕ cups) water

250 ml (1 cup) light brown sugar

250 ml (1 cup) coarsely grated carrots,
   firmly packed for measuring

30 ml (2 Tbsp) butter

5 ml (1 tsp) ground mixed spice

250 ml (1 cup) cake flour

5 ml (1 tsp) bicarbonate of soda

5 ml (1 tsp) baking powder

a pinch of salt

250 ml (1 cup) wholewheat flour

60–75 ml (4–5 Tbsp) chopped walnuts (optional)

2 ml (½ tsp) vanilla essence

Place the cake mixture, water, sugar, carrots, butter and spice in a large, deep saucepan, bring to the boil, then cover and simmer over low heat for 15 minutes. Cool completely before continuing with the recipe. Sift the cake flour, bicarb, baking powder and salt and stir into the cooled mixture in a large mixing bowl. Mix in the wholewheat flour, nuts (if using) and vanilla. Turn into a 20 x 9 x 7 cm loaf tin, first oiled and then lined, base and sides, with baking paper. Level the top and bake at 160 °C for 1 hour. Test with a skewer and, if done, leave to stand for a few minutes before inverting onto a rack. Remove paper and cool. **Makes 1 medium loaf.**

EASY WHOLEWHEAT BREAD with seeds and raisins

An any time nibbly bread that delights and fills up children and adults alike. It's quick to make, and goes with everything any time of the day. The raisins may be left out if serving with a savoury dish.

4 x 250 ml (4 cups) wholewheat flour
250 ml (1 cup) white bread flour
1 x 10 g sachet instant dried yeast
7 ml (1½ tsp) salt
90 ml (6 Tbsp) sunflower seeds
30 ml (2 Tbsp) sesame seeds
125 ml (½ cup) seedless raisins (optional)
30 ml (2 Tbsp) oil
15 ml (1 Tbsp) each molasses and honey, or all honey, or
all molasses*
about 500 ml (2 cups) very warm, but not hot water**
sunflower seeds, sesame seeds and poppy seeds
for topping

In a large bowl, mix both the flours, the yeast, salt, seeds and raisins. Stir together the oil and molasses and/or honey, and mix in well. Mix in 250 ml (1 cup) of the warm water. Slowly add the remaining water, or enough to make a soft and sticky batter – not sloppy, nor stiff. Oil the base and sides of a 26 x 9 x 7 cm loaf tin, then line, base and sides, with baking paper. Spoon in the bread mixture, using a damp wooden spoon to press in firmly and smooth the top. Sprinkle with the seeds in diagonal stripes, for a professional look, and leave in a warm place to rise until just over the top of the tin. In winter this could take as long as 1 hour. Bake at 200 °C for 30 minutes, then at 180 °C for 20 minutes. Leave to stand a few minutes, then turn out, remove paper and knock on the bottom – if it sounds hollow, it's done. Now cool on a rack or, if you want to crisp the sides, return to the switched-off oven, out of the tin and upside down, for about 10 minutes.
Makes 1 large loaf.

* Molasses adds colour, flavour, iron and minerals.
** The only pitfall in making this bread lies in using water that is either too cold or too hot – in either case the yeast won't rise. The water should be hotter than lukewarm but definitely not hot enough to make coffee. Practice will soon make perfect.

stirred WHOLEWHEAT AND YOGHURT BREAD

This wholesome bread, which was once so popular, seems to be somewhat neglected now in favour of crusty, savoury Italian breads – understandable, but a pity. However, here it is again as a reminder – easy as pie, and full of good things. Despite the raisins and nuts, it's great for sandwiches as it slices thinly without crumbling – and it also makes a lovely lunch, with avo and cottage cheese and greens. The quantity of bicarb might seem very small, but it is enough for the bread to rise, and using this minimum amount avoids that overtly bicarb flavour that often surfaces in breads made with this ingredient as a raising agent.

250 ml (1 cup) white bread flour

7 ml (1½ tsp) salt

5 ml (1 tsp) bicarbonate of soda

750 ml (3 cups) wholewheat flour

60 ml (4 Tbsp) wheatgerm

90 ml (6 Tbsp) seedless raisins

30 g pecan nuts, chopped (optional)

500 ml (2 cups) stirred Bulgarian yoghurt (not thick, spooning yoghurt)

15 ml (1 Tbsp) oil

30 ml (2 Tbsp) runny honey

water

sesame and poppy seeds for topping

Sift the white bread flour with the salt and bicarb. Mix in the wholewheat flour, wheatgerm, raisins and nuts, if using. Whisk together the yoghurt, oil and honey, stir into the flour mixture, then add just enough water to make a sticky but not sloppy dough – rinse out the yoghurt carton with 100 ml (⅖ cup) water and use as much of this as necessary – you might need it all. Stir hard until thoroughly combined, then turn into a well-oiled and baking paper-lined 26 x 9 x 7 cm loaf tin, patting in evenly. Lightly press the seeds into the top and, to prevent uneven rising, make a slight depression down the centre (it will, nevertheless, hump in the oven, but it will settle down later). Bake at 180 °C for 60–70 minutes, then leave to stand for 5 minutes before loosening the sides and turning out onto a rack to cool. **Makes 1 fairly large loaf.**

WHOLEWHEAT MINI-BREADS with fig preserve and goat's cheese

These sweetish little breads, looking for all the world like rocky brown muffins, are made in a trice and are just the thing for a filler at brunch, or for a trendy little breakfast with coffee. The minis, speckled with raisins and hinted with cinnamon, simply beg for a glistening, syrupy preserved fig alongside, with a disc or two of soft goat's cheese and a bowl of soft butter. These mini-breads could take the place of croissants when you're wanting a wholesome alternative. They're far more appealing than sliced bread, and quicker than yeast rolls.

250 ml (1 cup) white bread flour
5 ml (1 tsp) bicarbonate of soda
5 ml (1 tsp) baking powder
5 ml (1 tsp) salt
5 ml (1 tsp) ground cinnamon
750 ml (3 cups) wholewheat flour
90 ml (6 Tbsp) seedless raisins
30 ml (2 Tbsp) treacle sugar (or soft brown sugar)
30 ml (2 Tbsp) honey
20 ml (4 tsp) oil
500 ml (2 cups) buttermilk
milk for glazing
sunflower seeds for topping

Sift the white bread flour, bicarb, baking powder, salt and cinnamon into a large mixing bowl. Add the wholewheat flour, raisins and sugar. Whisk together the honey, oil and buttermilk; add to the flour mixture and stir until thoroughly combined. The mixture needs to be quite soft and sticky, and you might need to add a spoon or two of water (rinse out the buttermilk carton) so that it can easily be scooped into the muffin cups. Rather add too little than too much, though – the dough must not be wet and slippery. You will need large muffin cups (not paper cases) for these mini-breads – oil them lightly first and then divide the dough equally – don't try to make them flat, just leave them more or less as they drop. Brush the tops lightly with milk, sprinkle with sunflower seeds and bake at 180 °C for 25 minutes until well risen, firm, and rocky in appearance. Leave to stand for about 10 minutes before carefully removing to a rack to cool. Best served on the same day, with the figs and the cheese. **Makes 12.**

WHOLEWHEAT ROSEMARY AND GARLIC ring bread

Mixed in minutes, this herby batter is turned into a tube tin where it billows into a big, fat ring, and the aroma while baking will waft right through the house. This wholesome, moreish loaf slices well, and may also be baked in a regular loaf tin if preferred.

4 x 250 ml (4 cups) wholewheat flour*

250 ml (1 cup) white bread flour*

1 x 10 g sachet instant dry yeast

7 ml (1½ tsp) sea salt

30 ml (2 Tbsp) finely chopped fresh rosemary leaves

45–60 ml (3–4 Tbsp) chopped fresh parsley

3 cloves garlic, crushed

4 spring onions, chopped

30 ml (2 Tbsp) oil

30 ml (2 Tbsp) treacle sugar

about 600 ml (2⅖ cups) warm water

Mix all the ingredients, except the water, in a large bowl. Slowly stir in just enough of the water to make a moist but not sloppy batter. The water should be warmer than lukewarm, but far from boiling hot. Turn into a 22 x 9 cm tube tin, oiled and lined with baking paper – base, sides and funnel – even if it's a non-stick tin. Use a dampened spatula to spread evenly. The batter should reach halfway up the sides. Cover lightly with a cloth and leave to rise in a warm place until doubled in size – about 30–40 minutes, depending on the weather. Bake at 200 °C for 30 minutes, then reduce heat to 180 °C and bake for a further 20–25 minutes, until risen and browned. Leave to stand for a few minutes before turning out onto a rack to cool, using a spatula to ease it out if necessary. If baking as a loaf, use a 26 x 9 x 7 cm tin, oiled and lined, and do not cover when rising as the batter will stick to the cloth. It should rise to just over the top of the tin – add about 10 minutes extra to the baking time. Leave to stand for a few minutes before running a spatula round the sides to invert. Cool.
Makes 1 ring bread.

* For a somewhat lighter loaf, use 750 ml (3 cups) wholewheat flour and 500 ml (2 cups) white bread flour – in this case slightly less water is required.

quick-mix HERBED BUTTERMILK BREAD

This is a jumbo loaf, humped and crusty and plump with flavour. Easy to make, as everything is simply
stirred together – no rising time required – and it's super with soup or at a braai.
Best served slightly warm and thickly sliced.

500 g self-raising flour
250 ml (1 cup) wholewheat or brown bread flour
7 ml (1½ tsp) salt
5 ml (1 tsp) sugar
10 ml (2 tsp) dried mixed herbs
3 cloves garlic, crushed
125 ml (½ cup) chopped fresh parsley
4–6 spring onions, chopped
500 ml (2 cups) buttermilk
1 XL free-range egg
150–180 ml (⅗–¾ cup) water
grated pecorino cheese for topping

Mix all the ingredients, except the buttermilk, egg,
water and pecorino. Whisk the buttermilk with the
egg, add to the dry ingredients and stir to mix, then
rinse the empty buttermilk carton with the water and
add just enough to make a thick, sticky batter. The
mixture needs some hard beating with a wooden
spoon in order to combine, as it is heavy and dense –
but it should not be sloppy, so do not add more
water than is absolutely necessary. Turn into a
26 x 9 x 7 cm loaf tin, first oiled and then lined, base
and sides, with baking paper. Use a dampened
spatula to pat in evenly and sprinkle with pecorino,
pressing it in lightly. Bake at 180 °C for 1 hour – it
should have risen quite dramatically and be golden
brown in colour. Insert a skewer into the centre to
see if the loaf is done. Leave to stand for a few
minutes, turn out, remove the baking paper and
return to the oven for about 5 minutes to crisp the
sides, then remove to a rack. **Makes 1 very large loaf.**

CONVERSION TABLES

METRIC	US CUPS	IMPERIAL		CELSIUS (°C)	FAHRENHEIT (°F)	GAS MARK
5 ml	1 tsp	³⁄₁₆ fl oz		100 °C	200 °F	¼
15 ml	1 Tbsp	½ fl oz		110 °C	225 °F	¼
60 ml	4 Tbsp (¼ cup)	2 fl oz		120 °C	250 °F	½
80 ml	⅓ cup	2¾ fl oz		140 °C	275 °F	1
125 ml	½ cup	4½ fl oz		150 °C	300 °F	2
160 ml	⅔ cup	5½ fl oz		160 °C	325 °F	3
200 ml	¾ cup or ⅘ cup	7 fl oz		180 °C	350 °F	4
250 ml	1 cup	9 fl oz		190 °C	375 °F	5
				200 °C	400 °F	6
100 g	-	3½ oz		220 °C	425 °F	7
250 g	-	9 oz		230 °C	450 °F	8
500 g	-	1 lb		240 °C	475 °F	9
750 g	-	1¾ lb				
1 kg	-	2¼ lb				

INDEX